Generating Failure

A Cato Institute book

JUN 18 1990

Seattle Public Library

Please note the date this item is to be returned
and keep the date due card in the pocket.

Generating Failure
Public Power Policy in the Northwest

David Shapiro

University Press of America
Lanham • New York • London

Library of Congress Cataloging-in-Publication Data

Shapiro, David L.
Generating failure.

1. Electric utilities—Government policy—Northwestern States.
I. Title.

HD9685.U6A1457	1989	333.73'92'09795	89–5651

ISBN 0–8191–7238–3 (alk. paper)

To my grandchildren
Aaron, Allison, Evan, and Hillary

Contents

Foreword

Federal power policy, like a second marriage, represents the triumph of hope over experience. Although the initial objectives and authority of the major federal power agencies were somewhat different, the subsequent power records of those agencies are distressingly similar.

The Tennessee Valley Authority (TVA) was established in 1933 to provide multiple-purpose development of the Tennessee River system. This development was to include the generation, transmission, and marketing of hydropower, plus irrigation, flood control, and agricultural development. The Bonneville Power Administration (BPA) was established in 1937 for a more limited objective: the transmission and marketing of power from the Bonneville Dam on the Columbia River and, later, from all federal power facilities in the Northwest. BPA and the other power marketing administrators that were established later were specifically prohibited from financing and operating power-generating facilities.

The case for these federal power programs was based on a claim that public utilities could provide power at a lower cost than the alleged "monopoly" power rates of private utilities. Each of the federal power agencies was subject to the following power marketing guidelines:

- All power-specific costs were to be recovered from power revenues.
- Municipal and cooperative retail power utilities were to have preferential access to power supplied by federal agencies.
- And all nonpreference customers (private utilities and direct industrial customers) could be terminated on due notice if the forecast demand by preference customers exceeded the expected supply by federal agencies.

The record of these agencies would provide an interesting test of the case on which this massive experiment in social engineering was based.

As it turned out, few of the hopes and most of the fears about this experiment were realized:

1. Power rates to customers and in regions served by these agencies were maintained at a lower level than rates to other customers and regions. The lower rates, however, were due not to lower costs but to large continued federal subsidies in the form of direct appropriations, low-interest loans, and flexible amortization schedules on the outstanding debt. Moreover, the environmental record of TVA's coal-fired plants has been substantially worse than that of private utilities. Despite these large subsidies, both TVA and BPA power rates are now converging rapidly on the rates charged by private utilities.

2. These federal agencies have substantially exceeded their primary charter, to develop and market hydropower. About 90 percent of TVA's power is now supplied by coal-fired plants. In addition, TVA invested about $15 billion in nuclear plants without producing any power; three completed plants have been closed for safety reasons, other plants in various stages of construction may not be completed, and eight other scheduled plants were canceled.

BPA's record is similar, even though BPA is prohibited from owning any generating facilities. BPA promoted the building of five large nuclear plants by the Washington Public Power Supply System (WPPSS, now more commonly known as Whoops). However, BPA used an irresponsible billing procedure never approved by law. BPA and its customers now have the financial responsibility for three of these nuclear plants—only one of which is operating. The other two are not likely to be completed because WPPSS defaulted on $2.25 billion in bonds to finance those two plants, the largest default on municipal bonds to date. Most authorities think these plants will never be completed.

3. Our political system has been very protective of the federal power agencies, despite their flawed structure and management failures. Donald Paul Hodel, the BPA administrator most responsible for promoting the expansion of the WPPSS nuclear program, was later promoted to secretary of energy and secretary of the interior in the Reagan administration. In 1982, shortly after the formation of an interagency group to study the pricing policies of the power marketing administrations (a group that I chaired), Congress prohibited spending funds to continue this study. In 1986,

following a Reagan administration proposal to sell BPA, Congress prohibited the expenditure of funds to study the privatization of TVA or any power marketing administrations.

Although the Constitution authorizes the president to "require the opinion, in writing, of the principal Officer in each of the executive departments, upon any subject relating to the duties of their respective Offices," Congress has increasingly restricted the executive branch from spending funds to study controversial issues. The Reagan administration, for reasons that are less clear, did not challenge this unconstitutional restraint on executive powers.

This careful book on the history and problems of the Bonneville Power Administration summarizes only one example of a federal agency that has grossly exceeded its initial charter, at the expense of federal taxpayers and, ultimately, at great expense to the constituents it was intended to serve.

A final word of warning to government officials who have a responsibility to be informed about these issues: Do not read this book on the job; Congress's thought police may be watching. For the rest of us, this book should increase our outrage about the performance of at least one federal agency and about the attempt of Congress to suppress public study and debate of these issues.

WILLIAM A. NISKANEN

William A. Niskanen is chairman of the Cato Institute and was a member of the Council of Economic Advisers in 1981–85.

Preface

The generation and distribution of electric power in the Pacific Northwest has been a continuing source of legal and economic controversy for over two decades. Although controversy over electric power is not unknown elsewhere in the United States, the problems encountered in this region differ in nature and degree from those encountered elsewhere. Indeed, the region's problems have received widespread attention in both the popular and academic press. Particular attention has been given to the abandonment of two large nuclear power plants and the associated default on $2.25 billion worth of bonded obligations.

The various power problems of the Pacific Northwest remain far from resolved. In addition to the large number of legal and economic problems that have been inherited, new ones are still arising. The pervasiveness and duration of these problems arouse curiosity regarding the policies that have shaped and influenced power use in the region.

In particular, federal power policy comes under scrutiny because of its overriding importance in the Pacific Northwest. One of the two major multipurpose river developments of President Franklin D. Roosevelt's New Deal took place on the Columbia River. Since then, a federal agency, the Bonneville Power Administration (BPA), has been the overwhelming power presence in the region. Indeed, the agency's role was expanded significantly under a 1980 act of Congress. The history of local electric power development and use in the Pacific Northwest, therefore, is inextricably interwoven with federal power policy. Consequently, an examination of that policy is essential for understanding the region's problems.

A central imperative of federal power policy, both in this region and elsewhere, has been to encourage the distribution of federal power by publicly or cooperatively owned utilities. The policy does not mandate that power be denied to private utilities, but it does accord preferential treatment to publicly or cooperatively owned utilities. (Some of the intellectual currents leading to the public power movement are discussed in chapter 1. Here, it suffices to note only that the public power movement encouraged the intervention of various levels of government in the generation and distribution of electric power.)

The transmission network in the Bonneville area was constructed by the federal government to encourage the formation of not-for-profit electric utilities, particularly in Washington State. Preferential treatment for these nonprivate utilities was codified in federal statutes, beginning with the original Bonneville Project Act of 1937. These preference provisions have had pervasive effects on subsequent events in the region and have led to many of the economic and legal problems encountered in the disposition of the Bonneville power.

Although a mixed private/public pattern of distribution evolved in the region, severe problems later arose over legal rights to the federal hydropower. The preference provisions appeared to give the favored utilities the right to preempt the supplies of federal power that had been contracted to the private utilities. Obviously, new power supplies would be far more costly than federal hydropower, and disputes over the rights to existing federal supplies started to escalate in the 1960s. These disputes hampered the orderly introduction of new generating facilities that were needed to satisfy increasing demands.

BPA attempted to resolve these problems and preserve preference rights by establishing a program designed to introduce new supplies and average the costs among all of its customers. This enterprise encountered severe difficulties, however. BPA's program involved the participation of a municipal corporation, the Washington Public Power Supply System (WPPSS), in the building of five large nuclear plants. BPA was financially involved in three of the five plants. When two of the plants were abandoned, WPPSS defaulted on $2.25 billion of the bonded obligations that financed them. Construction on two of the other plants has been postponed, and there is little hope of resuming construction on them. The failure of BPA's program led to congressional passage of the Pacific Northwest Electric Power and Conservation Act of 1980, commonly called the Regional Power Act, which attempted to preserve preference rights while allowing for the economically rational introduction of new power supplies.

BPA's program provoked a seemingly endless stream of litigation. Much of this litigation has arisen out of the default on the bonded obligations of WPPSS. In addition, a great deal of litigation has arisen out of the 1980 act, including one case that has been decided by the U.S. Supreme Court.

Several academic studies of public policy have discussed the power problems of the Pacific Northwest. They have concentrated largely on the events leading to the default or on the planning impacts of the 1980 act. Little or no attention has been given to exploring the relationships between the original federal power policy of the 1930s and the various problems and controversies in the region. The following questions, for example, seem well worth addressing: What federal power policy was implemented in the region? How was that policy implemented over time? How is that policy being implemented now? Should that policy be continued in the future?

The absence of studies that fully address these questions is less surprising than the virtually universal acceptance of the idea of the beneficence of New Deal public power policy. This policy was adopted, after all, in the face of controversy that had continued into the 1950s. Standard histories of the New Deal era tend to treat public power advocates as the forces of good and private power advocates as the forces of evil. Indeed, supporters of private power are viewed in these histories as being in the thrall of private utility interests or at least as having exaggerated fears of socialism.

This uncritical acceptance of the goodness of public power has also permeated the academic policy studies of problems in the Pacific Northwest. At worst, BPA is seen as implementing worthwhile public policy badly.

This acceptance may be a case of history being written by the victors. In the Pacific Northwest, public power policy in one form or another did prevail over a purely private power policy, to a greater or lesser extent. However, these victories do not offer conclusive evidence that public power offered a superior mechanism for power distribution at the time that it was adopted, or that public power should be encouraged and furthered today.

It is easy to understand uncritical acceptance of the superiority of public power in the 1930s when New Deal policies were being implemented. At that time, popular opinion held that monopolistic and collusive excesses were occurring in many sectors of the nation's economy, particularly in the electric power industry. But the institutions surrounding power provision have changed markedly since then. The federal government enacted holding-company legislation, and most states have enacted rather stringent public utility regulation. Therefore, it now seems illogical at best to cite the historical "evils" of private power without reference to subsequent changes in order to grant superiority to public power.

In any event, the question of whether public power policy should have been adopted is a counterfactual one of only historical interest. What is important is to examine the way in which public power policy has worked in the Pacific Northwest and to analyze the extent to which it has contributed to the region's problems. The question of contemporary interest is whether public power policy should now be modified or discarded to address today's power problems.

This study seeks to explain why public power appears to have worked so badly in the Pacific Northwest. Two competing hypotheses could explain this poor performance. One is that the public power policy implemented was inherently flawed. In particular, the legal and economic controversies that evolved stemmed, almost inevitably, from the preference provisions of that policy. In addition, the failure of federal operations to cover costs tends to cast doubt on the basic premise of the public power movement that furnishing of power to rural areas could be effected while covering costs. In a phrase, public power policy in the area has been a failed policy in that it had no reasonable possibility of success no matter how well it was implemented.

The alternative hypothesis is that public power was and is necessary for the efficient performance of the electric power industry in the Pacific Northwest. In this view, the problems experienced there have resulted from seriously maladroit implementation of a worthwhile policy. The various inept actions of BPA and WPPSS lend some credence to this interpretation. This hypothesis can be described as one policy failure.

The position taken in this study is that the failed-policy hypothesis is the appropriate one. This position is based on the perception that the public power policy implemented in the Pacific Northwest was almost predestined to fail. For one thing, it was predicated on the dubious proposition that the failure to provide power for thinly populated areas arose out of the monopoly position of private utilities. For another, once federal hydropower supplies became oversubscribed, the severity of the preference provisions virtually guaranteed legal and economic controversy. It may be true that BPA, and especially WPPSS, made the worst of a bad situation. This study rejects the notion, however, that better implementation would have salvaged matters. The policy-failure hypothesis is therefore rejected.

Scope of Study

As noted above, the public/private power debate appears to have disappeared from the academic or policy literature. The time is propitious to reopen the debate. The situation in the Pacific Northwest offers a convenient opportunity to do so in light of the events that have occurred there. A critical examination of the Tennessee Valley Authority (TVA) and municipally owned systems would prove useful if further study were to be pursued. Also of interest would be an examination of public power policy implementation in other countries such as France and Great Britain.

The problem of generalizing from the effects of public power policy in the Pacific Northwest region is that the corpus of public power policy differs markedly from area to area. Greatly varying policies are subsumed under the broad rubric of "public power policy." At one extreme, such policy has been construed as requiring the comprehensive planning of all resource use affected by electricity—which is to say, almost all resource use. At the other extreme, such policy has been taken to mean no more than inducing publicly owned utilities to enter the power industry to countervail the monopoly powers of private utilities or combinations of them.

It follows that rather different institutional arrangements may all be consistent with the idea of public power policy. The state monopoly in France, for example, has used economically sophisticated pricing mechanisms whereby the rates charged bear a regular relationship to the costs of provision. BPA, on the other hand, has explicitly rejected such schemes and insists upon averaging costs among the customers within its region.

In sum, this study focuses on the public power experience in the Pacific Northwest and leaves the study of public policy in other areas for a later time or to others.

Outline of Study

The outline of this study is as follows. Chapter 1 discusses the origins of the public power movement in the United States and examines the movement's analytical bases; in addition, it provides a brief history of the development of public power policy in the Pacific Northwest. Chapter 2 traces the effects of federal power policy in the region up to the present time; the WPPSS bond default and events leading to the 1980 act play a prominent role in this narrative. Chapters 3 and 4 detail the economic and legal consequences, respectively, of public power policy in the region. Chapter 5 ties together the conclusions of the previous chapters and offers policy recommendations based upon them. The Reagan administration showed some interest in the privatization of some federal operations, and a specific proposal was made in regard to BPA's operations. This proposal is discussed and evaluated in the final chapter.

Personal Postscript

Although I did serve in the Department of Energy (DOE), which is now BPA's parent agency, I neither participated directly nor was otherwise involved in the administration or operations of BPA. The research leading to this study was begun as an analytical exercise for DOE's Energy Information Administration. Furthermore, I do not have, nor have I ever had, any direct or indirect association with the private or public electric power industry. My interest in the subject is purely academic.

Acknowledgments

My long-time editor, Esther A. Spachner, offered helpful editorial assistance in the early stages of this effort. The dean's office of the School of Business, San Francisco State University, typed an early version of the manuscript through the cooperation of Associate Dean Klaus Schmidt. Professor Lawrence Lee of the San Jose State University history department offered substantive contributions that are acknowledged specifically in the text, and a travel grant from San Jose State assisted my research greatly. Unbounded appreciation is due the Cato Institute and its editorial staff. Finally, my wife Caryl assisted in proofreading and other details of manuscript preparation. More importantly, she bore the considerable burden of living with me during the long and tortuous effort involved in the writing of the book.

1. Public Power Policy: The Controversial Origins

Public power policy as implemented in the Pacific Northwest has been an exceedingly important determinant of the pattern of electric power generation and distribution there. (This region consists of Oregon, Washington, Idaho, and the portion of Montana lying west of the Continental Divide.) One mandate of this policy not only has shaped the pattern of distribution but also has been the key factor in the various economic and legal controversies that have racked the region for over two decades: the mandate that publicly and cooperatively owned distributing utilities be given first rights to purchase federal power.

Public Power Policy: The Beginnings

The public power movement gained increasing political momentum in the first three decades of this century. Many specific programs were advocated by public power enthusiasts, the common denominator of such proposals being the necessity of the participation of government agencies in the generation and distribution of electric power. Otherwise, electric rates would be higher than would be the case without government participation. More important, it was argued, private utilities could not be relied upon to furnish power to rural and sparsely settled areas.

The economic significance of electricity grew during these three decades. The development of large river systems such as those in the Tennessee and Columbia river basins promised cornucopias of additional electric power. The public power advocates were insistent that these large supplies of power be distributed widely and cheaply, a goal that would not be achieved by private utilities pursuing their economic interests. Some form of ownership and control by nonprivate organizations was thought to be essential to ensure the wide distribution of low-priced power.

The movement drew upon many of the intellectual currents of the time, such as socialism and the progressive movement. These ideologies varied rather widely, but the common thread running through them was a desire for increased government intervention in private markets, particularly in markets for basic resources such as electricity. In addition, the adherents of these ideologies disagreed on what extent of government intervention was desirable. This dissension accounted for the wide variety of subpolicies that were implemented. At one extreme was a call in 1928—from the politically futile Socialist party—for "a publicly owned giant power system under which the federal government shall cooperate with the states and municipalities in the distribution of electricity to the people at cost" (Friedman and Friedman 1980, p. 311). At the other extreme was a demand for government intervention simply to provide the private utilities with the kinds of competition that could not be achieved by market forces or state regulation.

As the 1930s approached, electricity was in very wide use in the United States, particularly in the cities, but the country still lagged far behind western European countries such as Norway in rural electrification. "But on the countryside," according to one historian, "nine out of ten American farms in 1933 relied on gas engines, horses, mule and hand labor for power, and on kerosene lanterns for light" (Schlesinger 1960, p. 379). Farmers mobilized political pressures in their attempt to obtain electric power. Contemporary historians argue that public power legislation was adopted during the New Deal era because vast areas of the rural South, the plains states, and the Pacific Northwest had never been provided with central-station electric service. It was in these regions that the votes in Congress originated for the Rural Electrification Administration, for the Tennessee Valley Authority, and for the Bonneville and Grand Coulee projects in the Pacific Northwest (Fungiello 1973, p. 256).[1] The acknowledged political leader of the public power movement was Sen. George Norris, the independent Republican from Nebraska, who was supported for reelection by President Franklin D. Roosevelt in 1936.

Political support for public power was strengthened by the real or supposed malfeasance of the private power industry. The device of the electric power holding company in particular was criticized

---

[1] I am indebted to Professor Lawrence Lee of San Jose State University for pointing this fact out to me. Professor Lee also gave me valuable bibliographic and other assistance in the writing of this chapter. He is, of course, absolved from blame for the chapter as it appears.

by the public power advocates and by Roosevelt himself. Such holding companies held controlling interests in other power companies, although they may not actually have generated or sold electric power themselves. They were accused of shady or even illegal financial manipulations that were widely publicized when Samuel Insull, the head of one of the major holding companies, fled the country to escape prosecution. (He later was extradited, tried, and acquitted.)

President Roosevelt charged that "if it were not for the money pumped out of operating companies by holding companies, power rates to the consumer could be reduced everywhere in the country and the private firms would have nothing to fear from TVA" (Schlesinger 1960, p. 303).

By 1932, 13 holding groups were said to control three-quarters of the privately owned electric utility industry, according to Roosevelt's National Power Policy Committee. The three largest groups— United Corporation, Electric Bond and Share, and Insull—controlled some 40 percent (Schlesinger 1960, p. 304).

The allegedly monopolistic nature of the power industry led its critics to charge that private companies would not distribute power unless they could thereby make large profits. According to various historical accounts, the private power companies were wedded to a "high rate/low usage" concept (Morison 1965, p. 965; Schlesinger 1960, p. 374). Interpreted in economic terms, this observation means that the power companies were able to restrict output to elevate the prices of the power actually supplied.

In particular, these monopolistic practices of the private companies were thought to be responsible for their failure to supply power to farms and sparsely settled areas. There seemed to be relatively little concern by these critics about the supply of electric power for the nation's cities.

The public power movement gained momentum in the 1920s with proposals to construct multipurpose projects on river systems such as the Tennessee and Columbia to generate large amounts of hydropower (the electricity generated by falling water). This type of power was usually cheaper and cleaner than so-called thermal power derived from the combustion of such substances as gas, oil, or coal and was inexhaustible in the bargain.

One of the early public/private confrontations came over the development of the Tennessee River basin. Private industry sought to develop the electric power potential of Muscle Shoals, a 37-mile stretch on the Tennessee River with a drop of 134 feet over a geological dip. A dam had been constructed there by the federal government in World War I to produce nitrates for the production of munitions. In 1921, Henry Ford had offered to take over the Muscle Shoals facilities but had been vigorously opposed by public power advocates led by George Norris. Having claimed that, among other things, the Ford offer was grossly inadequate in price, the Norris-led forces were successful in blocking it. Later in the 1920s, Boulder Dam (later named Hoover Dam) was initiated during the Coolidge administration with relatively little controversy. Although a federal project, both public and private organizations contracted for the power, with no preference being given to either as the project evolved. "Hoover did not propose to admit creeping socialism into the federal household. The concept of 'partnership' in power between the federal government and private agencies became the regular Republican party gospel thereafter" (Merk 1978, p. 515).

TVA Power Policy

The development of the Tennessee River valley became one of the most lauded achievements of the New Deal. An independent government entity, the TVA was formed to plan, develop, and administer the federal undertaking in the area. The setting up of the TVA did fulfill the dreams of George Norris and the public power advocates. However, the implementation of the policy aroused a well-publicized controversy that illustrates the differing conceptions of public power policy already noted. A leading historian of public power policy has stated the basic controversy:

> Public power–conscious officials were themselves a complex lot motivated by diverse and sometimes conflicting interests. The extremists among them saw experiments like the TVA, rural electrification projects and Bonneville Dam as intermediate measures on the road to full-fledged public power. The moderates conceived of the New Deal power program as a "yardstick"—a public enterprise that would be competing with private producers and force them to bend more toward the needs of the consumers. [Fungiello 1973, p. 257]

Another writer has elaborated on the yardstick notion: "Federal power as a 'yardstick' for private utility rates and service reflected both a distrust of private utilities, which were often controlled by large holding companies far removed from local consumers, and a fundamental lack of faith in the ability to control utility excesses through regulation" (Blumm 1983, p. 241).

The more extreme group saw the TVA and holding-company legislation as the core of a program that ultimately would embrace the resources and power needs of entire regions. The more comprehensive planning role was espoused by an early TVA chairman, Arthur Morgan. He proposed turning the power resources of the river over to private industry as the most effective way to achieve his desired economic and social objectives. Morgan was exceedingly critical of David Lilienthal, his archrival, whose primary goal was inexpensive power at the expense of other objectives. The deepseated differences between the two men were aired publicly when Morgan published an article in the *New Republic* in 1937. Schlesinger summarized the article as follows: "He denounced, naming no names, men ruled by a Napoleonic complex, constructing essentially a war or social revolution designed not to come to terms with companies but to destroy them. It was wrong, argued Morgan, to treat all utilities as if they were run by buccaneers of the past" (Schlesinger 1960, p. 369).

It is true that the profound dispute between Arthur Morgan and David Lilienthal touched on many points other than whether private companies should distribute TVA power. There is some irony, nonetheless, in the fact that Morgan, a dedicated central planner, was willing to entrust power resources to private utilities.

Lilienthal vanquished Morgan and went on to head the TVA and become its revered guiding spirit during its early development. In fairness to Lilienthal, public/private antagonism on both sides thwarted many of the efforts to work out an accommodation between the TVA and the Commonwealth and Southern Corporation, the large electric utility in the TVA region. This utility was headed by Wendell Willkie, later to become Roosevelt's presidential opponent in the 1940 election. Willkie's intractability on some points was thought to stem from his belief that later elections would eliminate the public power "nonsense."

Lilienthal's goal of inexpensive power became the guiding spirit of the TVA, and the broader planning goals receded into the background. Whether the development of the valley could have been accomplished with private/public cooperation remains an unanswered—and now unanswerable—question.

The basic TVA act included a wide range of planning goals. In addition to the generation of power, the TVA was made responsible for flood control, navigation, and the manufacture and distribution of fertilizer. Also contemplated were other programs designed to raise the economic and social well-being of the people living in the river basin.

An important aspect of the TVA legislation involved the preference provision that came to assume great importance in subsequent events in the Pacific Northwest. This provision gives the first rights of purchase of federal power to publicly and cooperatively owned electric utilities. Sen. George Norris had fought for preference rights in the TVA region from 1920 to 1933. The underlying idea was to protect electricity users from private utility monopolistic exploitation. Were these utilities able to buy inexpensive federal power, according to the argument, they would restrict distribution to their most profitable marketing opportunities and would not supply the power to rural and thinly populated areas. The BPA history notes:

> The TVA Act expanded the concept of preference three ways.
>
> First, it included cooperatives. This paved the way for a thousand rural electric cooperatives across the country, which eventually provided support for the preference clause. The Rural Electrification Act of 1936 gives preference to public bodies and cooperatives in applying for REA loan funds. . . .
>
> Second, the TVA Act authorized construction of Federal transmission lines, thus giving potential preference customers direct access to the power.
>
> Third, the Act directed the inclusion of a 5-year pull-back clause in contracts with non preference utilities. *All three of these innovations became part of the Bonneville Project Act* [emphasis added]. [BPA 1981, p. 71]

The pullback, or cancellation, clause contained in contracts for federal power with private customers provides for the termination of these contracts upon due notice when the supplies of federal power are not sufficient to meet the demands of preference customers.

Public Power Policy in the Pacific Northwest

In 1932 there was great political enthusiasm in the Pacific Northwest for the federal construction of two multipurpose water projects on the Columbia River. The nation's economy was severely crippled by the Great Depression, which continued to worsen during that year. Two large potential dam sites were available for development. Voters in Oregon were pressing for a dam near Portland, while

Washington voters favored the site in the interior of their state.[2] (The Bonneville Dam was built near the first site and the Grand Coulee Dam at the second.)

The Democratic presidential candidate that year attempted to please the region's voters. Speaking in Portland on September 21, 1932, Franklin Roosevelt pledged "that the next great hydroelectric development to be undertaken by the Federal government must be that on the Columbia River" (Lowitt 1984, p. 57).

The statement may or may not have been purposely ambiguous. In any event, Roosevelt was reminded of his campaign promise by a senator and a representative from Oregon on May 5, 1933, two months after the president's inauguration. The BPA history states that after this reminder "Roosevelt knew that his campaign promise had been interpreted in Washington to mean construction of Grand Coulee Dam and in Oregon construction of the dam at Warrendale" (BPA 1981, p. 36). (The proposed dam at the Warrendale site was later moved to the present site of the Bonneville Dam.)

The Roosevelt administration redeemed the campaign pledge in Portland by initiating construction of the two projects in 1933. They were begun as New Deal emergency measures about two years before formal congressional authorization. More important, the projects were begun without resolving the problem of how the power from these dams would be distributed.

As the projects were being constructed, an intense and protracted political controversy arose concerning the distribution of power from the Bonneville Dam near Portland. (The decisions that were reached with regard to this project were later applied to the Grand Coulee project when it was integrated into the system.)

The partisans of public power sought to create an agency modeled after the TVA, to be known as the Columbia Valley Authority (CVA). Bills were introduced in Congress that would have enabled the proposed agency to administer Columbia River development and take control of the two dams from the constructing agencies, the Corps of Engineers (Bonneville) and the Bureau of Reclamation (Grand Coulee). The private power interests resisted this proposal

[2]Ordinarily, there is confusion between Portland, Oregon, and Portland, Maine. Similarly, Washington could refer to the state or to the nation's capital. Such distinctions would become tedious if used frequently. Therefore, in this study, Portland is used to refer to Portland, Oregon, and Washington is used to refer to the state— unless Washington, D.C., is specified.

and sought an alternative that would have served to deliver the power to private utilities. Another bill introduced in Congress called for the Bonneville project to be administered by the Corps of Engineers. Power would be sold at the generating facilities or, at most, two short trunk transmission lines would be constructed to Portland and its neighboring city of Vancouver, Washington. With such a plan, the private utilities in Oregon would have been the primary beneficiaries of federal power from this dam.

Public power advocates argued that such an arrangement would perpetuate the private power monopoly and serve to deny power to the small and geographically dispersed publicly and cooperatively owned utilities. These utilities could only reap the benefits of federal power if the government were to plan and build transmission lines and substations to parallel dam construction (BPA 1981, p. 47).

The relatively small and geographically dispersed publicly and cooperatively owned utilities would have been effectively foreclosed from access to federal power if the power were to be sold only at the point of generation or nearby. Financing would be hard to come by, particularly in the depths of the Great Depression. The absence of federal financing would give the electricity to the private utilities by default. Those companies, presumably, would deliver the power into their existing networks and sell the power to urban and settled areas. The goal of the public power movement to distribute power to farms and thinly populated areas would supposedly be frustrated.

In 1936, the voters of Oregon and Washington rejected proposals to have their respective states construct the transmission lines. Therefore, the issue had to be decided by the federal government.

There was much lobbying and congressional dispute on the various aspects of power control and distribution from Bonneville Dam. In addition, different federal agencies were vying for administrative control of the power. The questions of the construction lines were subjected to intense debate in Congress and among the agencies involved.

President Roosevelt summoned the congressional delegation of the Pacific Northwest to a White House conference in February 1937. He adumbrated four policy decisions that were to shape the development of the federal power in the region:

> 1. That power from the dam would be marketed separately from privately produced power.

2. That the publicly and cooperatively owned distribution systems would receive preference.

3. That the federal government, rather than private enterprise or local government would construct the backbone distribution system.

4. That a new civilian agency to market the power from the dam would be established within the Department of the Interior. [Fungiello 1973, p. 184]

The very critical decision of whether the rates should be uniform or should reflect transmission distance was to be vested in the administrator of the new agency. That agency was to be administratively housed in the Department of the Interior under the watchful eye of Secretary Harold Ickes. Ickes and Interior were thought to be far more sympathetic toward public power than the competing agency, the Corps of Engineers (Fungiello 1973, p. 184).

The day following Roosevelt's meeting with the congressional delegation, a bill was introduced in the House embodying the president's policy proposals. After further parliamentary debate and compromise, the bill passed Congress and was signed into law on August 20, 1937. Known as the Bonneville Project Act, the law delineated the parameters of federal power policy in the region.

Public power advocates have lauded the passage of the act as a great victory. In the words of the BPA history,

> The new law represented another milestone for Roosevelt, and, as it turned out, virtually the capstone for the New Deal power program. Key policies of the Act later became a nationwide marketing policy in the Flood Control Act of December 22, 1944.
>
> Basically, the Bonneville Project Act established the Bonneville Power Administration and serves as BPA's charter or organic law. The Act assigns responsibilities: the Corps of Engineers generates the power. The Corps installs and operates generators requested by the Administrator. The Administrator builds and operates transmission facilities, markets and exchanges power, negotiates power contracts and proposes rate schedules. FPC [Federal Power Commission, now the Federal Energy Regulatory Commission] makes the cost allocations and approves rates. These constitute the structural decisions of the Act." [BPA 1981, p. 63]

The act concerned itself only with the power generated by Bonneville Dam, which was constructed by the U.S. Army Corps of Engineers. This left open the question of the disposition of power from Grand Coulee Dam, which was constructed by the Bureau of Reclamation of the Department of the Interior. This problem was resolved without apparent legal controversy. In 1940, a Bonneville–Grand Coulee transmission line was placed in service. Shortly thereafter, Roosevelt signed an executive order directing BPA to market power from all federal power generating facilities in the region consisting of Oregon, Washington, Idaho, and the western part of Montana.

These developments in fact constituted a partial, but far from total, victory for the public power advocates. Federal construction of the transmission facilities to make power available throughout the region ensured access for the widely dispersed publicly and cooperatively owned utilities. The ability to distribute the power was ensured further by the formation of the Rural Electrification Administration, which subsidized construction of nonprivate facilities by making loans to them at below-market interest rates.

One important type of nonprivate utility that became extremely significant in Washington was the public utility district. "The PUD was an elective unit of local government whose boundaries generally coincided with an entire rural county. Endowed with substantial powers to borrow money, incur debt, levy taxes, and issue bonds, it was organized to market hydroelectric power on a nonprofit basis" (Fungiello 1973, p. 200). The various political conflicts over electric power in the region stemmed, in no small measure, from the battle for federal power between the private utility interests in Oregon and the PUD lobby in Washington.

Roosevelt did insist, however, that the operations of the new agency be self-supporting.[3] As Fungiello notes:

> While his enmity toward individual utility magnates and their creature, the holding company, was very nearly instinctual, Roosevelt also recognized that in selling power the federal government had to act in a commercial rather than an eleemosynary capacity. The guiding principle in financing the New Deal's power projects was to treat them as self-supporting enterprises, which, though not operated for profit, were expected to earn from revenues all proper charges against them. [Fungiello 1973, p. 258]

---

[3]This requirement appears to have been codified in a later enactment, the Flood Control Act of 1944. The requirement that BPA's operations be self-liquidating was also included in the 1980 act.

In addition, the TVA preference provisions noted earlier were incorporated into the Bonneville Project Act and in subsequent legislation concerning power in the Pacific Northwest, including the Regional Power Act of 1980. These provisions led to severe economic and legal difficulties in the region (see chapter 2).

Thus, the policies of public power advocates were carried to their logical conclusions. The federal government was mandated to finance a widespread transmission system that would distribute power to widely dispersed rural and thinly populated areas. But the federal agency was adjured to cover all the costs of generation and distribution. This mandate was not honored, as subsequent events reveal. In any event, let us examine some of the economic reasoning in support of public power.

Some Economics of Public Power

The creation of the TVA and BPA implemented public power policy in varying degrees. In both regions, considerable rural electrification followed, and this result appeared to validate the two basic premises of the public power movement: (1) the rural areas had been denied electricity because of the high rate/low use (monopolistic) policies of private companies, and (2) consequently, electricity could be furnished to these areas through government intervention at rates that covered costs. (Even the Socialist party called for the provision of power at cost.)

The validity of both premises underlying public power is seriously in doubt. The monopoly argument is difficult to evaluate. Some monopoly in the provision of electricity is almost inevitable. Economists term this situation "natural monopoly." As Richard Hellman has expressed the idea, "The crucial theoretical justification for the legalization of monopoly in the electric utility industry is the indivisibility of the massive physical investment. It would be economically inefficient and impracticable, the argument runs, to duplicate this plant" (Hellman 1972, p. 51).

But the mere existence of a natural monopoly does not warrant the conclusion that electric power will not be supplied in the absence of excessive returns. At the least, more information would be required to reach such a conclusion. This conclusion was the point, however, of an oft-told anecdote involving Roosevelt. "He often recalled the astonishment with which he first inspected at Warm Springs an electricity bill with rates four times as high as those at Hyde Park" (Schlesinger 1960, p. 381). It is not surprising that electric rates were lower at Hyde Park, in the Hudson River valley not far from New York City, than they were in Warm Springs, a remote hamlet in Georgia. It is entirely possible, and plausible, that the difference in rates reflected differences in costs and not in profit.

More generally, the private companies' disinterest in supplying power to rural areas in the Tennessee and Columbia river basins may have been based on their inability to earn a normal rate of return on investment. That is, private companies would not construct facilities unless their returns were likely to be greater than or equal to those they could earn elsewhere.

During the Great Depression, when public power policy gained its greatest impetus, such profitable investments were hard to come by. Indeed, the BPA history details the decline in private utility investment in this period:

> The annual investment in hydroelectric generation fell from $117.6 million in 1930 to $4 million in 1933, and transmission facilities from $145 million in 1929 to $16.1 million in 1933. . . . From 1930 to 1934 annual utility construction expenditures in Washington State plunged from $34.6 million to $1.73 million, Oregon from $9.55 million to $1.07 million, Idaho from $10.5 million to $0.41 million and Montana from $3.52 million to $0.32 million.

> The electric utility construction doldrums were part of the investment and employment vacuum that set the stage for federal power projects. [BPA 1981, pp. 31–32]

The thought process here is not entirely clear. Were the private firms culpable in their failure to supply power in the absence of profitable prospects?

Historian Arthur Schlesinger, Jr., appeared to answer this question in the affirmative. He conceded, more or less, that the provision of power by private firms could not have been profitable: " 'Unless rural service is worth more than it costs,' as one utility magnate put it, 'it should not be supplied'—and 'worth' was to be measured solely in terms of financial return" (Schlesinger 1960, p. 380).

Schlesinger was implying that private firms should be guided by considerations other than financial returns. But why should a private firm supply power if revenues fail to cover costs? Like other public power advocates, Schlesinger offered no answer to this question. Although a case can be made that a public agency should be guided by social benefits that are not reflected in financial returns, neither Schlesinger nor other public power advocates have done so.

In sum, it seems fair to conclude that the failure of private utilities to furnish power to rural and sparsely settled areas arose out of the inability to do so while covering costs. Public power advocates appeared to have argued that the private utilities required a substantial return in addition to costs in order to supply these areas. This became known in public power advocacy as the high rate/low use policy of private utilities.

Support for the High Rate/Low Use Argument

The analytical reasoning behind the high rate/low use argument is difficult to follow. Even conceding considerable monopoly power to the private companies, it should still be within their interest to supply thinly populated areas if it were marginally profitable to do so. With the ability to separate markets, the companies could charge higher prices to those users based on the higher costs, and they would be induced to do so if their costs could be covered. But the public power argument proposes that this will not be done and that the only remedy is active government competition. Richard Hellman has described the breakup of the monopoly of the private utility in the TVA region and the subsequent rural electrification:

> Shortly after the TVA Act in May 1933, the monopsony [single buyer] was broken by purchase of company transmission lines to the Muscle Shoals plant and by construction of others. The groundwork for breaking the monopoly was laid through preference for TVA power to municipalities and rural electric cooperatives (REC's); purchase of company properties by TVA and resale of distribution systems to municipalities and REC's; a TVA fund for financing these acquisitions or construction if necessary; a TVA transmission network; and construction of steam plants for an efficient power system. [Hellman 1972, p. 25]

The intervention by government agencies such as TVA and BPA did appear to lower the cost of power and to facilitate the desired rural electrification. As Alfred Kahn, a leading expert in the field of utility regulation, has written:

> But there is strong evidence in the public utility area that *competition between* the two systems of organization, like competition among private businesses, is highly conducive to improved performance. It may take the form of direct rivalry (for the patronage

of the same customers in the same market); or of competition-by-example (where comparisons may be drawn between the performances of private and public enterprises in serving their respective customers, in different markets); or by threat of total displacement (where the management of each is aware that voters are examining its performance with the possibility of substituting one system of control for the other). [Kahn 1971, p. 104]

The problem that troubled Kahn (and even Schlesinger) is the appropriateness of using the performance of publicly owned utilities as a yardstick by which to judge the relative public/private performance. Kahn continued:

There has been endless controversy over whether the numerous municipally owned and operated distribution companies (many of whom do their own generation of power as well) or the cooperatives that have been organized to supply power in rural areas, with the aid and encouragement of the Rural Electrification Administration, or the various Federal power projects like those in the Tennessee Valley are really fair "yardsticks" for determining whether private power rates are as low as they might be. Direct comparisons of rates do not, in fact, provide a fair test of relative economic efficiency: the taxes and costs capital for public and private companies differ in material respects. [Kahn 1971, p. 105]

Kahn proceeded to elaborate some of the economic reasoning involved:

The fact remains that there is intense rivalry between these public and private systems, far less in the form of direct competition in the market for the same customers than at the political level, along the lines already suggested. It is clear that the public power companies—most notably TVA—were able to take the risks of setting rates low and thereby to test their assumptions about the high elasticity of demand on the one hand and the downward slope of their long-run cost curves on the other—risks that private companies either could not take or, at any rate, could not be forced by the regulatory commissions to take. To what extent it was the example of TVA's experience, demonstrating that it was in their private interest in any event to reduce rates, and to what extent the fear that if they did not do so there would be other TVA's set up to take over their business, is not important. [Kahn 1971, p. 105]

Kahn drew heavily on the work by Richard Hellman, who argued that government competition is a more effective mechanism for keeping rates low than utility regulation by state commissions. Hellman presents a host of case studies in support of his thesis: "The cases demonstrate that utility company managements when exposed to government competition have lowered prices and gained sales. More crucially, their finances have met the regulatory test of attracting capital for expansion. In a number of cases, rates of return have risen and exceed those of comparable companies not under competition" (Hellman 1972, p. 228).

Besides the question of comparability of costs, two other issues remain. First, state utility regulation has changed significantly in the direction of stringency over the half-century since the TVA came into existence. Second, the marketing of electric power was in its relative infancy at that time. The primary market was for illumination, and power for space heating and other uses involving the production of heat by resistance coils lay far in the future. Competition with other sources of energy has also served to lower electricity rates. These facts leave open the present-day relevance of the Hellman argument. A practical question thus remains to be answered: Are the preference provisions still required to furnish the government competition formerly thought to be necessary by public power advocates?

Preference Provisions Controversy in the Pacific Northwest

The desirable extent of preference protection for the eligible customers of BPA was controversial. In 1936, the Roosevelt administration's Natural Resources Committee questioned the economic wisdom of the pullback or cancellation provision in particular. (This provision was described earlier with respect to TVA policies.) As quoted in the BPA history:

> The prior right of cities, public-utility districts, cooperative organizations, etc., to the use of electric energy should be recognized in the law and policies of the proposed organization (BPA). It is doubtful, however, if the cancellation clauses enjoined by congressional statute upon the TVA for contracts with private organizations will be wise in the case of the Pacific Northwest if, as we recommend, sufficient capital is made available to the corporation to install the additional generating units at Bonneville and Grand Coulee. [BPA 1981, p. 73]

The committee recognized that gaining the participation of private utilities might be prudent from a business standpoint:

If and when there appears to be an approaching exhaustion of the surplus electrical energy from these public works, and if Congress fails to permit the construction of river projects which will afford additional sources of electrical energy, then the cancellation clause might become appropriate. It is extremely important for the solvent operation of the corporation that all of the energy be utilized as rapidly as possible because the corporation's capital structure must include a large share of the total cost of the dams and if only a fraction of the power capable of being generated at these structures is used, capital charges will quickly eat up all the revenues and increase the early deficits so as to menace the soundness of the entire enterprise. What is necessary, therefore, is to safeguard the power operations so that the demands of public groups and cooperatives which may reasonably be anticipated may be amply satisfied while at the same time other users may be found who will aid in achieving a full utilization of these works at an early date. [BPA 1981, pp. 73–74]

These recommendations were ignored in the aftermath of Roosevelt's overwhelming victory in the 1936 presidential election as being overly conservative. The February 9, 1937, report of the President's Committee on National Power detailed the preference idea more forcefully and at greater length than had been done before or has been done since. The committee rejected the Natural Resources Committee's recommendation to eliminate the five-year pullback clause with the private utilities.

The debate over the preference provisions continued for some years, at least as late as 1946. A governor of Oregon argued, for example, that delivery of the federal power to private utilities would have enabled his state to best utilize the inexpensive power and attract industry to his state. Fungiello (1973, p. 202) indicts the governor and the business interests for viewing Bonneville from the perspective of economics, but the Bonneville facility had considerable difficulty in disposing of its power in its early years. Throughout its history the Bonneville Power Administration has had severe problems in repaying its obligations (see chapter 3). Perhaps a closer attention to economics could have alleviated some of these problems.

In any event, the entire distribution system financing and subsequent financial decisions of the power system of the Pacific Northwest were based on a profound distrust of private companies and a belief in the superiority of publicly and cooperatively owned distributing utilities. Charles McNary, the Republican candidate for vice president in 1940, expressed his distrust of private companies as follows: "All that the preference clause does is to prevent monopoly. It really should be called an antimonopoly defense" (BPA 1981, p. 74). A minor irony of history is that the presidential candidate on that ticket was Wendell Willkie, one of the leading opponents of the TVA in his role as chairman of the Commonwealth and Southern Corporation, the principal private utility combine in the TVA region.

BPA did sell surplus power to private companies, and these sales were warmly defended by public power enthusiasts with somewhat convoluted logic. The BPA history cites an academic economist, Martin Farris, in this regard:

> Among unintended effects, he [Farris] notes the large block of "residual" energy available at low rates to private utilities throughout BPA's early years. Preference customer energy purchases from BPA did not exceed those of private utilities until 1952. Farris suggests availability of this residual power enabled private utilities to avoid installing power plants, to reduce rates, strengthen their systems, and stop further sell outs of private power companies to public agencies. [BPA 1981, p. 76]

Public power partisans appear to have had it both ways. The public power policy denied power to the monopolistic firms. That policy served, however, to assist these companies and to lower their costs. The truth, in all likelihood, is that private companies helped avert a complete financial disaster for the federal projects in the Pacific Northwest.

The question of the relevance of public power provisions to modern times remains to be answered. The preservation of preference provisions played a large role in the controversy over the Pacific Northwest Electric Power and Conservation Act of 1980 (the Regional Power Act, for short). Public power spokesmen argued forcibly against the weakening of preference. Alex Radin, director of the American Public Power Association, expressed the following thoughts in the Senate hearings on the 1980 act:

> The preference clause has been repeatedly inserted in Federal statutes for marketing of Federal power as a means of insuring that Federal hydroelectric facilities are operated for the benefit of the general public.
>
> Goals of the preference clause are to (a) distribute the product of

public investment to the public through non-profit organizations
to the extent that citizens and communities wish to form them;
(b) provide anti-monopoly protection for consumers by assisting
competitive systems which establish a yardstick against which
one can compare utilities, and (c) support the opportunity for local
control over electric services. These historic aims have not been
diminished by time. [U.S. Senate 1978, p. 1072]

Radin's principal argument for preference retention does not
appear to be relevant to contemporary conditions despite the claim
that the historic aims have not been diminished over time. Whatever
the historical merits of the arguments, today's regulatory laws and
procedures obviate the need for government competition to protect
consumers from private utility monopolies. Nonetheless, the preference provision was nominally retained in the 1980 Regional Power
Act (although its protections were attenuated, as will be discussed
in the following chapter).

Conclusion

Public power policy has been controversial throughout its history
in the nation and in the Pacific Northwest. Public power policy
includes a wide variety of goals ranging from central national planning of power resources to the more limited objective of furnishing
inexpensive power to compete with private industry. The lack of
rural electrification in the 1920s and 1930s was blamed on the allegedly monopolistic and collusive nature of the private electric utility
industry. Political forces were mobilized on behalf of the public
power movement and led to the multipurpose federal projects in
the TVA and BPA regions early in the New Deal era.

The TVA represented a major victory for the public power movement in that it meant that a government entity had been given
broad planning authority for power use in a large region. In the
Columbia River region, the public power advocates won a more
modest victory after a protracted political controversy concerning
the distribution of power from Bonneville Dam. Private power
interests wanted the government to sell the power at or near the
generating facility, a plan that would have delivered the bulk of the
power to private utilities. Proponents of public power advocated
the establishment of a planning authority modeled after the TVA.
President Roosevelt dictated a solution intermediate between these
two extremes. The government would build extensive transmission

lines to facilitate the distribution of power to widely dispersed publicly and cooperatively owned utilities. Furthermore, these utilities would have the first rights of purchase to the federal power even to the point of preempting the supplies of power that had been contracted to private utilities. A government agency, housed in the Department of the Interior, would market the power of Bonneville Dam (and later of Grand Coulee Dam). However, the agency was denied the broad planning authority of a CVA. The system that evolved came closest to the "yardstick" approach whereby government agencies would offer vigorous competition to private utilities.

Roosevelt's dictate that the operations of the distributing agency be self-liquidating was codified in the authorizing legislation. This put to the test one of the basic premises of the public power movement: the proposition that power could be supplied to rural and thinly populated areas while covering costs.

Subsequent events tended to refute this proposition. This is not surprising given the weakness of the analytical support for public power. It is doubtful that the denial of power to these areas arose out of the monopolistic motivations of the private utilities. A more likely explanation is that it was not economically feasible for the private utilities to supply this power. This point is conceded, in effect, by Arthur Schlesinger and other public power advocates.

In any event, the decisions made in the 1930s set the pattern for the public/private mixed system in the Pacific Northwest and served to create many of the problems that later evolved. The following chapter focuses on the myriad problems that arose out of the imperatives of public power policy, primarily the preference provisions.

2. Preference Policy and Its Effects

The preference provisions pertaining to federal power caused little problem for many years after the completion of the Bonneville and Grand Coulee Dams. Indeed, the principal problem faced by BPA, the federal marketing agency, in the early 1940s was to find customers for the inexpensive federal power. Demands for the large increment of power were not available. The region was relatively unpopulated, and the Great Depression had not yet ended. The national press characterized the two dams as "white elephants," suggesting that they were not useful projects. In such a situation, the preference provisions were of no consequence.

The problems of disposing of the power were greatly simplified by the onset of World War II. The demands for fabrication of aluminum grew, owing to the metal's importance in military aircraft manufacture. The production of aluminum requires large amounts of electricity in order to convert bauxite ore into the metal. The federal government encouraged the location of aluminum manufacturing in the region to supply electric power to the region's aircraft industry. Indeed, BPA entered into direct contracts with the aluminum firms rather than marketing the power through public or private utilities.[1] The contracts did contain the pullback preference provisions but, given the exigencies of the war and the excess supply of power, these provisions caused little concern at the time.

---

[1]BPA itself, in its official history, and other defenders of public power make much of the contribution of Bonneville power to the war effort. This power did facilitate the production of aluminum that was used in making combat aircraft. Power was also shipped to the secret installation at Hanford, Washington, that produced nuclear materials for weaponry. However, this contribution to the war effort validates the public power argument only to the extent that the Bonneville and Grand Coulee dams would not have been built, at least at that time, without the participation of the federal government. The contribution of the war effort in no way justifies the assistance of the federal government in the financing of distribution systems. Certainly the power would have been available for the war effort without these distribution systems.

Problems Related to New Power Supply

The perception that the supplies of federal hydropower were inexhaustible was altered in the 1950s with the onset of the Korean War. In the meantime, the demands for electricity in the region and in the nation had grown significantly in the postwar era. Utility planners began to realize that alternative sources of power would be necessary to satisfy the future demands for electric power in the region. Proponents of public power attempted to afford BPA a key role in the development of new power supplies. But BPA had been denied the authority to construct new generating facilities. Rep. Henry Jackson of Washington introduced legislation in 1951 to give BPA limited authority to operate a fuel-operated plant in southeastern Oregon where the BPA transmission system terminated. In 1958 Sen. Richard Neuberger of Oregon introduced a bill proposing that BPA finance and build thermal plants. These bills did not become law, however.

In 1953 President Eisenhower reopened the public/private power dispute in his inaugural address. He outlined a "partnership policy" in which public agencies and private firms would cooperate in the development of power generating facilities. This program was not notably successful, but it did trigger strong lobbying opposition by the public power interests. The idea gained currency that Eisenhower planned to sell TVA, the leading federal public power installation, to private interests. Such a move "was seen as a direct threat to BPA as a federal entity and that meant that the privileged status of preference customers such as the PUD's was threatened" (Anderson 1985, p. 43).

This potentially alarming development led to efforts in the region to form a publicly owned joint operating agency to replace BPA if it were privatized. (A proposal to privatize BPA was made much later, during the Reagan administration, as will be discussed in chapter 5.) The advertisement promoting the agency's formation (1956) argued that "if Eisenhower carried out his threat to sell BPA, the association would have a public power agency in Washington (state) to buy out every line and substation" (Anderson 1985, p. 43).

The Formation of WPPSS

The system was formed on January 31, 1957, and was called the Washington Public Power Supply System. The original WPPSS consisted of 17 public utility districts (PUDs) from Washington State. Membership in the organization expanded and contracted over the years. In 1984 WPPSS consisted of 19 PUDs and the four cities of Richland, Seattle, Tacoma, and Ellensburg.

This organization came to play a key role in the events that followed in the region. One of its advantages was that it was organized as a municipal corporation. As such, it was entitled to preference under federal power law. It was also entitled to have the income from its bonds exempt from federal income taxation.

The fledgling agency was called upon to construct the small Packwood hydroelectric plant in Washington State. This project went rather well, and the agency was called upon to participate in another proposed power plant. The government decided to construct an additional nuclear reactor at Hanford in eastern Washington, which was the site of a World War II reactor. The excess steam power from this facility could be used to generate electric power. A protracted fight ensued over the disposition of this power. A compromise was reached whereby privately owned utilities received half of the facility's output.

> The role of BPA was to subsidize the cost of the plant through an exchange agreement under which utilities exchanged their share of the project power for equal values of BPA's less expensive hydropower. In effect, the exchange agreement allowed BPA to purchase power, a function specifically denied to BPA in 1937 when it was created, in 1949 when Congress rejected the idea of a CVA [Columbia Valley Authority], in 1951 when Senator Jackson introduced legislation for BPA to build and operate coal plants in Oregon, and again in 1958. [Leighland and Lamb 1986, p. 188]

Both the Packwood hydropower and Hanford nuclear plants turned out reasonably well, and WPPSS began to play an increasingly important role in the development of new power facilities in the region.

During the 1960s, the growth of power demands prompted still further efforts to construct thermal facilities. The anti–public power Eisenhower administration was replaced by the friendlier Kennedy and Johnson administrations. A Joint Power Planning Council, composed of the region's facilities and chaired by BPA, started plans to facilitate construction of large nuclear and coal-fired plants.

The Hydrothermal Program

In 1968 Stewart Udall, secretary of interior, approved a so-called hydrothermal program, originally formulated as a planning document. In 1969, the council refined the list with a 10-year program of specific plants with specific sponsors. The list included seven large thermal plants, three of which were to be large nuclear plants to be built by WPPSS. The program was approved by President Nixon in 1969, but the lack of statutory authority for BPA to construct generating facilities served as an obstacle to implementation of the program. The obstacle stemmed from the fact that the preference utilities that composed WPPSS lacked the ability to raise capital to finance construction of facilities. The preference utilities had little or no collateral to pledge for the sale of bonds. Their principal assets were the rights to buy power from BPA. Their participation in the hydrothermal program would have been rendered meaningless by their inability to raise capital. New power supplies could only have been financed by privately owned utilities. This would have diminished the role of the preference utilities in power provision in the region. It would also have impelled the preference utilities to accelerate their exercise of the preference pullback provisions of federal power legislation. Not incidentally, BPA would have been denied a role in the expansion of generating facilities to supply the increasing power demands of the region. The resolution of these problems was accomplished by an ingenious device known as net-billing.

Net-Billing

Net-billing evolved out of ordinary accounting procedures that are used almost universally in the operation of electric power networks. The smooth operation of such a network requires the exchanges of power, transmission, and related services from its users. Financial debits and credits must accrue out of these exchanges. BPA had employed net-billing to balance its accounts with its customers, as do other power networks. The amounts owed to BPA by its customers could be offset against the customers' obligations rather than paying the amounts owed in cash. The procedure, devised by BPA's power manager, Bernard Goldhammer, followed the precedent set in the construction of the Hanford generating plant. BPA exchanged its hydropower for the more expensive thermal power and passed the losses on to its ratepayers. But Goldhammer's procedure brought BPA more directly into the construction process. All of the costs of construction of the portion of the facilities that would generate power for preference customers would accrue to BPA by means of the net-billing procedure. These costs would have to be passed on and averaged among all of the agency's ratepayers, thereby increasing their rates.

Goldhammer was challenged by congressmen during an appropriations hearing for 1970–71, but the procedure survived despite its dubious legality in skirting the statutory proscription against BPA ownership of generating facilities. (A curious aspect of the matter was that Congress never gave formal approval to the procedure. The approval came in the form of the passage of an appropriations bill that included the costs to be sustained on account of net-billing.)

Goldhammer's ingenious scheme converted this simple accounting procedure into a mechanism that would enable BPA to finance thermal generation facilities despite the legal proscription against its doing so. The preference utilities were given the right to offset their construction costs for thermal generating facilities against their obligations to BPA for power received. These utilities could combine with other utilities, public or private, but only the preference utilities would have their expenses of construction offset against their obligations to BPA. BPA's obligations were on a "take-or-pay" basis; that is, the costs of the investments by preference utilities would be offset regardless of whether the plants ever delivered power. This point is important in view of the subsequent fates of the net-billed plants.

BPA's Use of Net-Billing

The key to BPA's use of net-billing is the manner in which it defrays these costs. Under law, BPA must pass on the costs of these obligations to all of its customers because the agency is required to cover all of its expenses. (Whether statutory requirements have actually been followed is discussed in chapter 3.)

If revenues from power sales are insufficient to cover the total costs of operation, BPA's rates have to be raised to comply with the congressional mandate. BPA's practices in this area, however, are to apply the method known as average-cost pricing; that is, it averages these additional costs among all its customers without reference to the additional costs of supplying particular customers.

The following is a simple numerical example that demonstrates the process without going into great detail. Suppose that preference utilities and nonpreference customers are each buying 1,000 units of power from BPA at $1 per unit. Also suppose that the preference utilities add 100 units of capacity at a cost of $2 per unit and net-bill these costs to BPA. BPA then averages these costs among all of its customers, including the preference utilities themselves. BPA's total costs now amount to $2,200 (2,000 units at $1 each plus 100 units at $2 each), and the average cost of BPA power is now about $1.05 per unit ($2,200 divided by 2,100).

Under BPA pricing practices, the rates for both classes of customers are set at this amount, $1.05 per unit. Without averaging, the nonpreference customers would still be paying $1 per unit but the preference customers would be paying about $1.09 (1,000 units at $1 each plus 100 units at $2 each; $1,200 divided by 1,100 is about $1.09). With averaging, therefore, the nonpreference customers are paying more for their power but less than the $1.10 per unit they would have to pay if their supplies of project power were preempted (900 units of project power at $1 each plus 100 units of incremental power at $2 each; $1,100 divided by 1,000 is $1.10). And the preference customers are also paying more than if they had preempted the power rights of the nonpreference customers but less than the incremental costs of the power.

Although the preference customers may appear to have gotten the worst of this bargain, such a conclusion can be tempered by three factors. First, preemption rights of the preference customers could be subjected to a determined legal attack, as will be detailed below. These attacks could be repulsed, but not without considerable expense. Second, the time would come, despite the preemption rights, when additional supplies would have to be introduced by the preference utilities, which would then have to sustain all of the incremental costs. The net-billing stratagem makes possible the orderly introduction of new supplies with the ability to gain cross-subsidization from non-preference ratepayers. Accordingly, the costs of introducing new supplies are thereby attenuated considerably. An important consideration was that a growing controversy over the exercise of the preference rights was forestalled.

GAO Objections

The General Accounting Office made little objection when the procedure was originally instituted, but later it did express some decided reservations.

> BPA's use of net-billing to acquire plant capability was concurred in during appropriations hearings for 1970–1971. It constituted an important supplement to BPA's charter—as a marketer of federal

hydropower—one which perhaps deserved more scrutiny than it received. Originally, the Congress regarded net-billing as a convenient way to settle accounts between Federal power marketing agencies and their customers. Net-billing had been used before the 1970's to balance the amounts owed to and by BPA in its various arrangements with customers for electric power sales, transmission and related services. The new use of net-billing was different and clearly distinguishable from the previous use. BPA was not offsetting moneys owed it for power sales with services it received. Instead, it was paying for the right to receive a share of output from a power plant built by a third party. This transaction did not involve services related to the day-to-day operation of the system but concerned the acquisition in installments of an ownership interest in generating capacity. [General Accounting Office 1979, p. 4]

Implementation of Net-Billing

The net-billing procedure, coupled with the successes of WPPSS's participation in the Packwood and Hanford plants, gave strong impetus to the hydrothermal program. Projections of future demands in the region indicated that large increments to the region's generating capacity were highly desirable if not essential. (The fact that these forecasts exaggerated the future demands did not become known until some time later.)

The program got started with the construction of a coal-fired plant at Centralia, Washington, under the co-ownership of a private utility, the Pacific Power and Light Company, and several publicly owned utilities. In Oregon, the Portland General Electric Company built the Trojan nuclear power plant with a 30 percent co-ownership by the Eugene Water and Electric Board. The latter's portion of the construction cost was financed by net-billing.

The program then moved on to three large nuclear plants to be built in Washington. WPPSS was chosen to construct these plants based, presumably, on the organization's "successful" efforts with regard to Packwood and Hanford. Some rather important points were overlooked, however. First, the Packwood plant was a hydroelectric plant that offered no experience in constructing and operating a nuclear plant. Second, as David Myhra pointed out, the Hanford experience was not particularly relevant.

> Nearly everyone missed one major point about the WPPSS/Hanford experience. WPPSS had not built the reactor itself, but had only built and operated the generating portion of the facility, the

part that turned steam from the nuclear reactor into electric power. WPPSS had no experience in building or operating nuclear electric plants. The significance of this would become apparent later. [Myhra 1984, p. 11]

Finally, the three new nuclear plants were built on far larger scales than the two nuclear plants undertaken in the region. The Hanford plant had a capacity of 430 megawatts, and the Trojan plant (which did not involve WPPSS) a capacity of 339 megawatts. The three nuclear plants to be constructed by WPPSS had capacities of 1,250; 1,100; and 868 megawatts, respectively.

These factors notwithstanding, the three plants were begun under the names of WNP 1, 2, and 3. The net-billing procedure was employed to finance the proportions of the plants' capacity that were owned by preference customers. All of the capacities of plants 1 and 2 were owned by preference utilities, while 30 percent of plant 3 was owned by private utilities. The three plants were estimated to cost about $1.61 billion (Leighland and Lamb 1986, pp. 8, 9).

The region's planners, evidently buoyed by the success of the net-billing procedure, went ahead with what came to be called phase 2 of the hydrothermal program. (Construction of the first three plants was phase 1.) The economic necessity of these plants was supported by the still exaggerated forecasts made by a trade organization, the Pacific Northwest Utilities Conference Committee (PNUCC), and endorsed by BPA.

Impediments to the use of the net-billing procedure had arisen, however. First, a ruling by the Internal Revenue Service removed an important advantage of having WPPSS carry out the construction. Prior to the ruling, the bonded obligations of WPPSS were exempt from federal income taxation because it was organized as a municipal organization under the laws of Washington State. But in 1972 the IRS ruled that the exemption would not apply if more than 25 percent of the power from the plants was assigned to nonexempt purchasers, which included BPA (Myhra 1984, p. 23).

A second blow to net-billing was the skyrocketing costs of project construction. The capital needed to build the original plants rapidly exceeded the amount that could be supplied by net-billing.

Early in 1973 BPA estimated that by 1981 the revenues derived by the sale of federal hydro to preference customers would amount to $145 million. But the annual cost of the thermal plants built under HTPP [Hydro-Thermal Power Program] would have amounted to $135 million over the net-billing limit of 85 percent. [Anderson 1985, pp. 86, 87]

Anderson continues:

The problem, then, was financing the additional plants. The formulators of Phase II came up with a fiscal replacement for net-billing known as a "participants' agreement." Each utility that signed such an agreement would be participating in a project by taking a portion of the project's debt in exchange for a respective share of the plant's output. The difference between the Participants' Agreement for the Phase II plants and the underwriting contracts that public utilities had signed for WNP 1, 2, and 3 was that participants in Nos. 1–3 were not directly responsible for the projects' debts. The Participants' Agreement had the effect of cutting out BPA as the power broker with ultimate responsibility for paying off borrowed construction funds and associated debt interest. [Anderson 1985, p. 90]

Phase 2

Nevertheless, the planning for phase 2 pushed ahead. The events surrounding the institution of this phase take on great importance in view of its disastrous denouement. BPA's articulate and aggressive administrator, Donald Paul Hodel, took a central role in promoting the ill-advised phase 2. (Hodel went on to become secretary of energy and secretary of the interior, in turn, in the Reagan administration.)

BPA first pledged an auxiliary role in the implementation of phase 2. This support was foreclosed by a dispute involving the Alumax Metal Company of Oregon. BPA was forced to prepare an environmental economic impact statement, a very lengthy and involved procedure.[2]

---

[2]According to BPA's official history, "BPA's participation in Phase II of the hydro-thermal program was challenged in connection with a court suit involving the power sales contract with the Alumax Pacific Corporation's proposed aluminum reduction plant in Hermiston, Oregon. The court ordered BPA to prepare an environmental impact statement (EIS) on the entire BPA program on the socio-economic aspects of the Alumax plant location and on the contracts relative to Phase II of the Hydro-Thermal Program" (BPA 1981, p. 276). Having reviewed this document as part of my duties at the Department of Energy, I can state that the economic analysis it contains is negligible.

With or without the auxiliary support, the publicly owned utilities were extremely reluctant to sign the agreement to participate with WPPSS in the construction of WNPs 4 and 5. They feared that they would be forced to pay for power that was not delivered. These "take-or-pay" contracts (called "hell-or-high-water" contracts in the region) specified that the individual utilities were liable for their share of the plant construction costs whether or not they delivered power. In the event that the plants failed to deliver power, the ratepayers of these relatively small utilities would have their rates increased to pay for the "phantom power" from the plants. (The legal controversy over these provisions is discussed in chapter 4.)

Hodel and BPA persisted in promoting the program. In 1974 Hodel wrote a letter to the recalcitrant utilities to promote the program. The key paragraph of that letter stated:

> Any utility which needs additional resources in the mid-1980's will need to enter these Participant's Agreements with WPPSS at this time. Only by utilities signing these agreements can these generating plants be constructed on the schedule required to meet loads of Northwest utilities after July 1, 1983. [General Accounting Office 1982, p. 14]

These efforts were still not successful. After a lapse of about two years, Hodel took even stronger measures to have the utilities sign these agreements. He was apparently urged on by President Nixon's secretary of the interior, Rogers Morton, who was Hodel's superior.

> On June 24, 1976, BPA issued Notices of Insufficiency to all its preference customers. In essence, these notices changed BPA's legal obligations to its preference customers after 1983. Existing BPA power sales contracts allow BPA seven year's notice to limit its obligations to meet the future load growth of its customers. After July 1, 1983, therefore, BPA's obligations to its preference customers will be limited to any amount of firm power determined by an allocation formula contained in each contract. *From then on, each utility will be obliged to seek its own resources to meet future growths* [emphasis added]. [U.S. Senate 1979a, p. 91]

Anderson observed:

> At best the notice of insufficiency was premature until more sophisticated forecasts could be made to corroborate those of PNUCC. At worst, it was tantamount to a threat to the public-

utility holdouts to sign the Participants' Agreements or risk
brownouts, if not blackouts, seven years hence. [Anderson 1985,
pp. 93–94]

The drastic medicine was extremely effective. Eighty-eight participating publicly owned utilities signed up within a month. The
two most notable holdouts were the cities of Seattle, Washington,
and Eugene, Oregon.

Taken together, the 1974 Hodel letter and the 1976 notice of
insufficiency raised the specter to the small and medium-sized
publicly owned utilities of having to raise expansion capital to meet
load growth, or demand increases.

Hodel's actions were strongly criticized over the years, particularly as the enormity of the disaster of phase 2 became apparent.
But he had been under strong bureaucratic pressure at that time (as
detailed by Anderson). In addition, Secretary Morton had authorized the issuance of the notices. Hodel was supported in his actions
by the forecasts of the PNUCC, although it seems somewhat strange
that a major federal agency would rely on statistical estimates from
other agencies.

But even taking these factors into account, it is difficult to excul-
pate Hodel from blame in the ensuing disaster of phase 2. The
utilities placed under duress were relatively small and under the
management of rather unsophisticated people. Similar considerations were also applicable to the management of WPPSS. These
unsophisticated managers were faced with the loss or curtailment
of preference power, the lifeblood, so to speak, of their operations.

Whatever the merits or origins or justification of the preference
clause, the rights to this power were the only real asset that these
utilities possessed. Indeed, they had been promised by federal
functionaries in the early days of BPA that the Columbia River was
analogous to a seam of coal that would never be exhausted. The
threats of the diminution of these supplies in the face of expected
increases in power demand by the organization charged with pro-
tecting their rights were matters of extreme gravity to them. Hodel
clearly exploited these fears to the utmost in his zealous pursuit of
phase 2.

The fears of the publicly owned utilities were probably intensified
by other effects of the preference provisions that were making
themselves felt during the decade of the 1970s. In 1973 BPA stopped
furnishing "firm power" to the privately owned utilities. (Firm

power is more or less guaranteed; nonfirm power is furnished only if stream conditions allow.) During that decade it became apparent that BPA could not renew the contracts of industrial customers as their contracts expired in 1981 and 1991 without additional power. These problems could only be exacerbated by diminishing the supplies of even the preference customers. The possibilities of legal and political confrontations among the three groups of BPA customers (preference utilities, privately owned utilities, and industrial customers) became more likely as the decade wore on. The hydrothermal programs, including phase 2, appeared to offer the only solution to these fears and problems.

In any event, phase 2 was under way, and the construction of two large nuclear plants was begun. WNP 4 and 5 had capacities of 1250 and 1240 megawatts, respectively.

Breakdown of Phase 2

It soon became apparent that WPPSS had little or no capability to carry out the formidable task of constructing large nuclear generating plants. Managerial difficulties abounded and, indeed, WPPSS became something of a managerial horror show.

Cost overruns grew to Brobdingnagian proportions. The original cost estimates of about $4.1 billion escalated to about $23.8 billion in 1981. The press began referring to WPPSS by the nickname "Whoops," which became entrenched as a satiric sobriquet. Subsequently, several writers detailed the various misfeasances, malfeasances, and nonfeasances of the WPPSS (Anderson 1985; Leighland and Lamb 1986; Myhra 1984). One of them has summarized the managerial problems as follows:

> Critics blame managerial stupidity and bungling for most of WPPSS' problems. In addition, WPPSS has been plagued by lawyers who wrote contracts whose legality had never been tested in court, investment houses eager to sell bonds and earn commissions, and a Board of Directors composed for the most part of farmers, ranchers, and small businessmen who held part-time political office and were utterly lost in the megabucks world of nuclear electric economics. [Myhra 1984, p. 11]

The cost overruns and managerial problems of WPPSS became known to the financial community, and sources of funding dried up. In January 1982, Moody's, the bond rating service, suspended ratings on WNP 4 and 5. That same day, a study commissioned by the Washington State legislature concluded that the region might not need the two plants before the year 2000 (Myhra 1984, p. 111).

The two contemporaneous developments presented an unappetizing choice to the managers of WPPSS. Funding was not available to continue construction of these two plants. They were faced with the choices of "mothballing" the plants, that is, spending the money to preserve them in a condition such that they could be reactivated at a later date, or of terminating the plants without further expenditure. WPPSS sought to avoid this choice by bringing these plants under the auspices of the Regional Power Act, then pending. If these plants could have been covered by the act, a mechanism akin to net-billing, called billings-credits, could have come to the rescue. As with net-billing, the costs of these plants would have been assumed by BPA and averaged among its customers. Continued construction or, more likely, mothballing could have taken place. WPPSS was not able to obtain this source of funding, however. It had no choice then but to terminate the two ill-fated nuclear plants.[3]

The problems of WPPSS were even more severe. Funds were not available to maintain the payments on the $2.25 billion of bonded obligations. In July 1983 WPPSS had to declare a formal default on its bonded obligations. This default triggered the largest municipal bond default in U.S. history. A tremendous amount of litigation followed (discussed in chapter 4).

Phase 1

The revised forecasts and cost overruns also affected WNP 1, 2, and 3, which did enjoy the benefits of net-billing. "Postponement" of construction of WNP 1 was followed by a similar action regarding WNP 3 after about 76 percent of that plant had been completed. The private utilities that owned 30 percent of WNP 3 contested the postponement in court. (The status of this legal controversy is discussed in chapter 4.) WNP 2 has been completed and is in commercial operation. It was delayed, however, and the costs of the plant were far more than planned.

Search for New Solutions

The net result of the failures of the hydrothermal programs was that the legal problems arising out of the preference provisions

---

[3]This termination resulted in the largest abandonment of nuclear plants in history as of that time.

arose anew. The pullback provisions were now more likely to be exercised in this failure of the program to provide the promised supplies of new power. The threatened exercise motivated the non-preference to find legal remedies to obtain improved rights to the federal hydropower. The three antagonistic interest groups threatened to bring their legal artillery into play. BPA's inability to solve the legal and economic problems with its hydrothermal programs motivated the interested groups to turn to Congress for a legislative solution.

There were three competing groups with legal claims:

Preference Customers

This group, consisting of PUDs, electric cooperatives, and municipalities seemed to hold the paramount rights to the federal hydropower by virtue of the preference provisions including the pullback rights. Understandably, they were zealous in the safeguarding of these rights because of their economic significance. They could only be persuaded to support any weakening of these rights by the promise of resolving the problems of new power supply.

Farm and Residential Customers of Private Utilities

Private utilities supply almost 50 percent of the electric power in Oregon, Idaho, and western Montana, but only about 20 percent of the power in Washington. The lack of access to federal hydropower resulted in significant rate disparities for utilities customers.

Residential ratepayers in Portland, for example, paid much higher rates than ratepayers in Vancouver, Washington (a suburb of Portland located on the Columbia River). In 1978, for example, a homeowner in Vancouver served by the Clark County PUD paid $11.10 for 1,000 kilowatt-hours of electricity per month, while a homeowner in Portland served by the Portland General Electric Company paid $27 for the same amount. In other words, the customers of the private utility were paying almost two and a half times as much for power as the customers of the PUD.

The farm and residential customers of the private utilities generally paid higher prices for existing supplies of power and faced the prospect of even higher prices as their supplies of BPA power were preempted. They could mitigate the price increase by finding a way to avail themselves of the benefits of the preference provisions.

To reduce these rate disparities, Oregon developed a legal mechanism to give the members of this group legal rights to preference power. These rights were not restricted under federal power law to any given set of preference customers at any time. There was no restriction on new preference utilities being formed and thereby becoming entitled to preference rights. Oregon, therefore, enacted a statute that took advantage of this preference loophole. This statute created a state Domestic and Rural Power Authority (DRPA), which was to purchase federal hydro energy and resell it to those Oregon residents who were being served by private power companies. These residents would then enjoy the lower costs of federal hydropower.

Although legal challenges to this procedure were expected, the prognosis for the success of this strategy appeared excellent. Idaho considered such legislation, and Montana and Washington indicated that they would attempt to follow suit if the strategy were successful (U.S. Senate 1979a, p. 92).

This strategy, if successful and if pursued in all four states, would have deprived the original preference customers of a great deal of the economic benefit accruing to their rights. The pool of preference power would have been shared with a much larger group of users and would have accelerated the necessity of introducing new power supplies for the original customers.

Industrial Customers

BPA sold power directed to several industrial customers, as noted earlier. The practice started during World War II when these firms were drawn to the area by the extremely low price of electricity. About 94 percent of these sales are to firms that manufacture aluminum. The remainder is sold to other metal manufacturers and to firms that produce paper.

The termination of the BPA contracts would have forced these firms to seek alternative sources of power. The obvious alternative source would have been the electric utilities in whose service areas those firms were located. There was no basis in current utility law for denying these industries service, nor for supplying them service at a discriminatory price (U.S. Senate 1979a, p. 93).

The importance of this is that many of these firms are located in Washington and in the service area of the preference utilities. Were BPA to terminate the contracts of these firms, they would immediately apply to their local electric utility for service.

Were the industrial firms able to compel power deliveries from the preference utilities, there would be an additional depletion of the fixed pool of federal hydropower. If this depletion were added to the depletion occasioned by the Oregon-type strategy to make private utility power users preference customers, the situation confronting the original preference customers would have been extremely serious indeed. They would inevitably be faced with much higher costs of power from the new sources of power that would have been required much earlier than otherwise.

The three interest groups lobbied vigorously in Congress to promote their interests. After protracted legislative wrangling and disputation, in 1980 Congress passed the Regional Power Act (Pacific Northwest Electric Power Supply and Conservation Act).

The Regional Power Act of 1980

Congress debated and considered the proposed act for about three years. Sen. Henry Jackson of Washington played a key role in shepherding the legislation through the Senate by using his influence as chairman of the Energy Committee. Apparently, he induced President Jimmy Carter to appoint his legislative aide, Sterling Munro, to be the administrator of BPA in hopes of facilitating passage of a bill that would resolve the Pacific Northwest's power problems. The legislative wrangling continued during the late 1970s until the bill was passed in 1980. Separate bills were introduced in the House and in the Senate. Five sets of hearings were held both in Washington, D.C., and in cities in the Pacific Northwest.[4]

The principal stumbling blocks to the resolution of the controversies were the preference provisions and the extension of BPA's role as manager of the region's power resources. Local interests welcomed BPA's financial assistance but opposed the loss of local control over the region's power resources. The preference customers feared any diminution of their preference prerogatives. Any real or imagined weakening of the preference provisions was bitterly opposed by public power interests, both in and outside the region. There was concern that any weakening of the preference provisions in the Pacific Northwest would set a legal precedent for weakening similar provisions in other parts of the nation. The legislative wrangling was complicated by the active participation of a very powerful congressman, John Dingell of Michigan, who chaired the Subcom-

[4]U.S. House 1978, 1979a, 1979b; U.S. Senate 1979a, 1979b.

mittee on Energy and Power of the Committee on Interstate and Foreign Commerce at the time and took an active role in formulating the House bill under consideration. His particular concern was the preservation of the region's fisheries resources.

These various controversies had not been resolved at the time of the national election in November 1980, which retired President Carter and reversed the partisan control of the Senate from Democratic to Republican. The long-standing controversies over the proposed act were quickly resolved in the aftermath of the election. That same November, the Senate, still under Democratic control, passed a bill intended to resolve the variegated power and associated problems in the Pacific Northwest. There was a bill pending on the matter in both houses, as mentioned above. In such a situation, the different bills are usually reconciled in a conference committee composed of delegates from the two houses. On November 17, however, the Senate passed the House version of the bill intact, thereby avoiding a time-consuming conference. The bill was sent to the lame-duck president, Jimmy Carter, who signed it into law on December 5.

The passage of an act to resolve the economic and legal problems of electric power supply in the Pacific Northwest required the harmonization of three major competing interest groups: customers of private utilities, the metal industrial firms, and the original preference customers. Some benefits had to be conferred on these groups and some costs exacted from them. (The literature of public choice economics sometimes terms these benefits and costs the exchange of currencies.)

Benefits for Customers of Private Utilities. The 1980 act conferred the greatest benefits on the farm and residential customers of the private utilities. The privately owned utilities became preference customers to the extent that their power was delivered to the appropriate ratepayers. This feat was accomplished by a rather complicated exchange mechanism that amounted to little more than a laundering operation to provide federal power to these users.

BPA sells the private utilities an amount of power that satisfies the demands of their farm and residential customers. In exchange, BPA buys back an equal amount of power at the utilities' average system cost. Invariably, BPA's rate is the lower of the two rates because BPA's cost includes federal hydropower priced at its original cost, which is much lower than thermal power introduced later.

The costs of the private utilities are heavily weighted by the cost of thermal power. The benefits of the exchange must be passed through directly to the farm and residential customers involved, except in Montana. The price reductions were to be introduced gradually after the passage of the act.

The purpose of the exchange mechanism is to give the farm and residential customers of the private utilities the benefits of the lower costs of federal hydropower. On the other hand, the rates of the preference customers have to be raised. For example, if BPA is supplying 1,000 units of power to its customers at an average system cost of $1 per unit, BPA begins to exchange 100 units of power with the private utilities, which have an average system cost of $2 per unit. The rates of the preference customers then have to be raised if BPA is to use its power rates to cover its expenses.

The following is a numerical example, with simplifying assumptions, of this process. If all the costs of the exchange are passed on to the preference customers, their rates would rise about 10 percent. BPA's costs for the 1,000 units of power are now $1,100, and this averages about $1.10 per unit. The reality is far more complex than this but the point remains that the preference utilities would have to sustain some additional costs.

The act does provide a limit on the extent that these increased costs can be passed on to the ratepayers of preference utilities. The preference utility customers are protected in whole or part from rate increases on this account.

The departure from public power policy, nevertheless, was dramatic. Some of the customers of the much-feared private power firms were able to purchase power generated by federal projects at rates that may approach those of the original preference customers. In some sense, the preference provisions have been salvaged by weakening them. The alternative evidently appeared much worse to the preference customers, and they were dragged reluctantly into the compromise.

Benefits for Metal Companies. For the industrial companies, the paramount benefit of the Regional Power Act was the assurance of continued supplies of power from BPA. This assurance made it unnecessary for these companies to turn to their local preference utilities for service. However, they had to pay a fairly steep price for this assurance. The act required that they pay for the increased costs to the original preference customers of carrying out the exchanges for the first five years following passage of the act. After that time, they were to be protected against rates deemed inequitable in relation to the rates charged by the preference utilities to their industrial customers. The metal companies, in a very restricted sense, became preference customers, although with far less benefit accruing to them than to the farm and residential customers of the private utilities.

Benefits for the Original Preference Customers. Of all parties involved, the original preference customers probably received the fewest net benefits from the Regional Power Act. Their awareness of this fact is reflected in the voluminous reports from congressional hearings on the bills. The lobbying group for the public power utilities made several appearances before congressional committees and expressed the concerns of its members over the dilution of preference provisions. Ultimately, the preference customers extracted several concessions in return for agreeing to the act's passage. They obtained a pledge in the act that the preference provisions would remain in full force after the act passed even though there was some obvious weakening. The preference utilities did obtain a provision that provides that any judicial interpretation of weakening could not be applied elsewhere in the nation. The most important concession obtained, however, was a limitation on the price increases that could be imposed on the original preference customers: their rates were to be no higher than they would have been in the absence of the act, subject to some modifying conditions. This protection is embodied in a so-called rate-cap provision contained in Section 7(a)(1) of the act.

The Rate-Cap Provision. The rate-cap provision was to become effective on July 1, 1985. Until that date, the preference utilities were to be protected against any rate increases arising out of the sale and exchange of power with the private utilities. The industrial firms were required to absorb those costs during this period. After July 1, 1985, their rates were to be kept in some sort of parity with the industrial customers of the preference utilities, so that the preference customers could conceivably be faced with having some of the exchange costs passed on to them. (The numerical example given earlier shows how these costs will rise.) To guard against this contingency, the act provides that the rates of the preference customers and federal agencies will not exceed what they would have

been had BPA not engaged in the power sales of purchase trans-
actions with the privately owned utilities. The rate cap can be raised
to take account of the hypothetical possibility that the preference
utilities were furnishing power to the industrial firms within or
adjacent to the utilities' service boundaries during the 1985–90 time
period.

The rate-cap provisions have led to litigation in the 1980s. The
preference customers' protection against rate increases depends on
what is assumed about the costs of serving the industrial firms in
the areas adjacent to the service areas of the preference utilities. It
is not surprising that the hypothetical calculations were contested
in court.

The preference provisions were weakened by these legal mach-
inations, but the immediate challenges to the industrial firms and
the ratepayers of private utilities were headed off. The preference
customers, along with the other classes of customers, did gain a
satisfactory method of introducing new supplies at reasonable costs.

Ownership Provisions. One key aspect of the Regional Power Act
of 1980 is that it codified BPA's ability to acquire and own generating
facilities, in clear contravention of the Bonneville Project Act of 1937
and succeeding legislation. The 1980 act offers a somewhat disin-
genuous disclaimer of an ownership role, as follows:

> In acquiring resources under Section 6, the BPA administrator
> may not own or construct any generating facilities. Acquisition
> will be accomplished by contract to pay for (1) the capability for a
> specific amount of power from a utility's system, or (2) power
> associated with a generating source, or a group of resources, or
> (3) a load reduction associated with a conservation measure. [BPA
> 1981, p. 88]

The disclaimer is obvious doublespeak. The clear intention of the
act is to accord BPA ownership rights. The legislative history of the
act reveals the doublespeak in the following quotations:

> BPA has no authority to own or construct power resources, and
> the proposed legislation does not grant this authority; it does,
> however, permit BPA to purchase the output or capacity of power
> resources that are owned or constructed by other entities.
>
> A second type of purchase arrangement is generally used when
> the power resource in question is not yet constructed. The owners
> planning to build such a resource may offer to sell an ownership

share in the project, or, alternatively, a share of the resource's planned capacity. In either event, the purchaser is obligated to pay its percentage share of the project's construction and operating costs for its share just as if the purchaser were a part owner.

The long-term purchaser is really equivalent to a part owner of the resource since the purchaser will receive the right to a certain percentage of the power for the life of the resource and will pay only the actual costs of the resource. It is fair that the purchaser assume its percentage share of the risks.

Purchase of capability by placing the purchaser in a quasi-ownership status also permits the purchase(r) to exercise effective oversight on resource management, construction and operation. A mere purchaser of power would have no opportunity. [U.S. House 1980, pp. 38-39]

The BPA ownership role begun under the net-billing program was codified and expanded in the act by means of a device called billings-credits. Billings-credits expanded the net-billing device in at least two particulars. First, BPA could acquire generating facilities for any of its customers. By comparison, under the net-billing procedure, generating facilities could be acquired only for preference utilities. Under the 1980 act, though, such facilities could be acquired for other BPA customers.

Second, facilities that are not conventionally considered as generating power could be acquired by billings-credits. For example, under the act, BPA could finance devices that conserve power. The amount of power conserved is considered as having been newly generated. BPA was also permitted to acquire renewable resources such as small hydropower facilities installed by residential and small commercial customers. Finally, the act permitted BPA to acquire major resources such as thermal generating plants on behalf of utilities, public or private, under certain conditions.

Rather unusual results can occur with the use of billings-credits. In the case of major resources, the acquiring utility has legal title to the generating facility, just as it did in the case of net-billing acquisitions. The utility, public or private, can offset the cost of the entire facility against its obligations for power from BPA. The costs of these facilities are averaged among all customers of BPA, as in the case of net-billing acquisitions. Under the net-billing procedure, however, the acquiring utilities must be preference utilities, which were unlikely to have other sources of supply. The billings-credits permitted under the act appear to extend the arrangement to all utilities in the region, including those unlikely to be purchasing all of their power from BPA. This provision implies that nonpreference utilities can avoid a large proportion of the costs that would otherwise accrue back to them under the averaging procedure described earlier. These costs would consequently be passed on to others.

Similar problems can arise from acquisition of power by means of the installation of conservation facilities. The utility introducing the conservation devices can reduce the cost of power to its customers, and the savings can repay the cost of the installation. The difference is picked up by BPA. Such utilities then offset these costs against their debts to BPA. Once more, these offsets are averaged among all users, including the utility enjoying the savings. There is no minimum amount the utilities must purchase from BPA. Conceivably, a utility could buy an amount equal to offset the costs of conservation devices and buy no additional power against which to offset these costs. In such a case, all of the costs will be shifted to other users, while the benefits will be enjoyed by the utility's customers.[5]

The Northwest Power Planning Council

During congressional debate over the Regional Power Act, its opponents expressed the fear that BPA's proposed intrusion into the ownership sphere would allow a federal agency to exercise economic hegemony over electric power use in the Pacific Northwest. Efforts to counter this hegemony would be difficult and costly. Certain economic interests in the area sought some sort of veto power over BPA's activities. Such a view was particularly important, given the transformation of BPA's role in power allocation.

The act resolved this problem by creating a locally appointed body, the Pacific Northwest Electric Power and Conservation Planning Council (the Northwest Power Planning Council, for short), to share planning authority with BPA. The council is made up of eight members, two each being appointed by the governor of each state in the region: Oregon, Washington, Idaho, and Montana. (Although Montana is sparsely populated and only a part of the state lies in the region, it was afforded equal representation on the council.) Complex voting rules were instituted to protect individual

[5]These are hypothetical possibilities, of course. The acquisition of generating facilities must be sanctioned by a plan approved by the council that is described in the following section. Whether or not these possibilities will, in fact, occur will depend on the decisions of that council.

states from majority rule, that is, a simple majority of the council does not suffice.[6]

The council was granted a very important role in the allocational process in the region. It was charged with formulating a plan for management of the region's electric power and allied resources. It was required that the plan provide for management of electric power resources, including conservation measures, and also a plan for the management of the region's extensive fishery resources. The plan must be submitted to BPA, which must concur in the plan and implement it.

A plan mandated by the Regional Power Act was published on April 27, 1983, and offered the comprehensive planning required by the act (Northwest Power Planning Council 1983). An amended version of the plan was published in 1986 (Northwest Power Planning Council 1986). BPA has circulated a draft of the council's 1986 power plan, but final responses are not available as of this writing.

According to the act, BPA, not the council, has final responsibility for managing the region's electric power resources. This management involves safeguarding the environment that could be adversely affected by electric power development. The council can recommend but only BPA is empowered by the act to implement the plans presented by the council. The act did not include a mechanism to reconcile differences between the two agencies. The council could, for example, submit a plan to BPA that would be rejected. The act does not specify how such a conflict would be resolved. Presumably, such a legal impasse would have to be returned to Congress for resolution.

Another legal objection was raised in the hearings before Congress. This objection arises out of the so-called appointments clause (Article II, Section 2) of the U.S. Constitution, which requires that important federal officials be appointed by the president with the "advice and consent of the Senate." The council members are taking an important, if somewhat undefined, role in directing the use of federal resources; that is, the power resources of federal projects including those acquired by net-billing or billings-credits. But these officials are neither appointed by the president nor confirmed by the Senate.

---

[6]The power plan, described below, must be approved by a majority of the council appointees, which includes at least one voting member from each state with members on the council, or by at least six members of the council.

Summary and Conclusion

The preference provisions helped shape the pattern of distribution of electric power in the Pacific Northwest, particularly in Washington. More important, the provisions helped ensure that formidable legal and economic problems would arise over the introduction of new power supplies in the region. The solutions to these economic and legal problems all involved circumvention of the preference provisions. BPA instituted its hydrothermal programs that attempted to introduce new supplies and to average the incremental costs among all of its customers. The failure of these programs to resolve the region's problems led to the passage of the Regional Power Act of 1980, which codified and extended the circumvention of the preference provisions.

The hydrothermal programs not only failed to resolve the problems addressed but they also generated a profusion of litigation. The bond default arising out of phase 2, in particular, led to multitudinous lawsuits, most of which are still pending. The Regional Power Act, in turn, has generated litigation of its own.

Whether the preference provisions were justified historically is now moot. At issue is whether the continuance of these provisions is warranted, particularly in view of their adverse economic consequences. Are the original considerations that led to the preference provisions still relevant a half-century later? Are the preference provisions necessary to ensure the widespread distribution of electric power to the nation's farms and other users of electric power? Are the preference provisions necessary to break the monopoly powers of the larger electric trusts? To ask these questions in this fashion, of course, is to answer them.

The issue of how to counter the monopoly powers of private power companies is hardly important at this time. The combined forces of the federal Public Utility Holding Company Act, the powers of the Federal Energy Regulatory Commission (formerly the Federal Power Commission), and pervasive state-by-state regulation keep these monopoly powers well in check.

The events associated with public power policy in the Pacific Northwest and the Regional Power Act of 1980 are fraught with irony. The act has served to greatly expand the roles of public agencies such as BPA and the regional council. Indeed, the roles assigned to these two bodies by the act come very close to that proposed for the Columbia River Authority a half-century ago.

Despite its disclaimers to the contrary, the 1980 act does involve BPA in a variety of ownership functions. The failures of public power policy as well as the failures of BPA's planning ventures have resulted in BPA being rewarded with an augmentation of its authority and responsibilities. It has been transformed from a passive wholesaler to an active central planner. What is more, the BPA administrator who was the architect of the disastrous phase 2 of the hydrothermal program, Donald Paul Hodel, has been rewarded first with one cabinet post and then another.

3. Economic Consequences of Public Power Policy in the Pacific Northwest

One of the critical issues concerning the financial practices of the Bonneville Power Administration is whether its operations have been self-liquidating as required by various congressional enactments. (As noted in chapter 1, Roosevelt insisted that this be the case.) The original Bonneville Power Act of 1937 states the following:

> It is the intent of Congress that rate schedules for the sale of electric energy which is or may be generated at the Bonneville project . . . shall be drawn having regard to the recovery of the cost of producing and transmitting such electric energy including the amortization of the capital investment over a reasonable period of years. [Bonneville Project Act of 1937 (16 U.S.C. 832)]

(Ironically, these words are quoted in the 1986 BPA annual report over a photograph of President Roosevelt signing the 1937 act.) The act does not further define the phrase "amortization of the capital investment over a reasonable period of years."

> Subsequent legislation, the 1974 Federal Columbia River Transmission System Act (16 U.S.C. 838g) and the 1980 Pacific Northwest Electric Power Planning and Conservation Act (16 U.S.C. 839e(a)(1)) requires Bonneville to set rates for selling federal power and transmitting nonfederal power to recover the amortization of the federal investment over a reasonable period of years. Further, Bonneville is directed to set electric power rates at the lowest possible level consistent with sound business practices. [General Accounting Office, 1983, p. 1]

If BPA's operations have not been self-liquidating, it follows that the electric power consumption in the Pacific Northwest has been subsidized by taxpayers in all regions of the nation. Illegality aside, this would negate the basic tenets and premises of the public power movement, which hold that the costs of providing power can be covered by the revenues of publicly owned utilities. Recent studies provide strong evidence that significant subsidization of BPA operations has taken place and continues to take place now.

Legal Proscription of Subsidies

The central argument of the public power movement has always been that electric power could be and would be supplied more cheaply and widely by publicly owned utilities than by private companies. The public power advocates have not based their case on the absurd notion that the rate advantages of public entities would be achieved by subsidies from the taxpaying public. Indeed, the public power advocates have denied, continuously, the necessity of such subsidies. The supposed rate advantages of public power, according to these advocates, would be obtained by operating an electric power system on a nonprofit basis. The lowering of rates would flow from the elimination of monopoly gains that were allegedly extracted by private companies.

These gains were thought to arise from the high rate/low usage policy supposedly followed by private companies. The publicly owned utilities would supply power to all users who were willing to pay the costs of provision. Sparsely settled areas, went the public power argument, would be supplied if monopoly profits were not insisted upon. It never conceded that subsidies from the general taxpayers would be required to provide this service.

The original Bonneville Project Act of 1937, as quoted at the beginning of this chapter, set down the guidelines for recovery. But the term "amortization" was not defined further in the act as noted above. The legislative history of the act shows, however, that Congress intended that debt amortization be delayed only if the dam's entire output could not be sold (General Accounting Office 1983, pp. 1–3).

The additional criteria were added by the Flood Control Act of 1944, which directed that electric power marketed by Bonneville be marketed "at the lowest possible rates to consumers consistent with sound business principles," but the term "sound business principles" remained undefined. (Presumably, it implies that all the costs of providing power must be covered.)

All operations of BPA were funded by Congress from BPA's inception until 1974. A change in this procedure was made that year with the passage of the Federal Columbia River Transmission Act, which dictated that the funding for Bonneville's transmission system be provided by borrowings from the U.S. Treasury. The act authorized BPA to issue obligations to the Treasury and have outstanding at any time up to $1.25 billion of bonds, notes, or other indebtedness bearing interest and having terms and conditions comparable to those prevailing in the market for similar utility debt instruments. (This limit was doubled to $2.5 billion by the Regional Power Act of 1980 and, still later, an additional $1.25 billion was added for conservation purposes.) Appropriations to BPA are still made for construction and replacement of Corps of Engineers and Bureau of Reclamation generating facilities.

BPA reacted to these legal requirements by stating a repayment policy that is described in annual reports. The highlights of the policy with regard to electric power are stated by BPA as follows:

Repayment Policy

> BPA's repayment policy is considered in determining its revenue requirements and rate levels. This policy, based on BPA's interpretation of laws and Department of Energy regulations, required that FCRPS [Federal Columbia River Power System] revenues be sufficient to:
>
> 1) Pay the cost of obtaining power through purchase and exchange agreements.
> 2) Pay the cost of operating and maintaining the power system.
> 3) Pay interest on and repay the outstanding revenue bonds sold to the Treasury to finance transmission system construction, conservation, and fish and wildlife.
> 4) Pay interest on the unrepaid investment in power facilities financed with appropriated funds. (Federal hydroelectric projects are all financed with appropriated funds, as were BPA transmission facilities constructed before 1978.)
> 5) Pay with interest, any outstanding deferral.
> 6) Repay the power investment in each Federal hydropower project within 50 years, after it goes into service (except for the Chandler Project, which has a legislated repayment period of 66 years). [U.S. Department of Energy, Bonneville Power Administration 1987]

BPA Repayment Practices

The BPA purports to have complied with the above legal requirements, as evidenced by the following quotation from the agency's

1982 annual report: "BPA has paid its own way with interest since 1937 when it was created by Congress. It has been self-financing since 1974 when Congress passed the Federal Columbia River Transmission Act. BPA is required by law to repay the federal investment in Northwest power facilities with its revenues. *BPA is not supported by public funds*" [emphasis added] (U.S. Department of Energy, Bonneville Power Administration 1983).[1] However, the assertion that BPA is not supported by public funds is sharply at variance with BPA's history of repayments.

The following brief history of BPA's repayments is taken from two GAO reports (General Accounting Office 1981, p. 21; 1983, pp. 1–3; all quotations are from these two reports).

In its second annual report, for fiscal year 1939, BPA used an annual amortization schedule (computed like a home mortgage with annual payments) to rebut charges in the national press—by publications such as *Collier's* magazine—that its projects were "white elephants." In that report, "Bonneville predicted that it would exceed a $4.1 million amortization requirement by an average of $3.4 million annually and pay off the full Government investment, plus interest, in 15 years."

In its FY 1944 report to Congress, BPA stated that it was adopting business principles governing repayment whereby its accounts would "reflect the application of revenues in much the same way as private industries apply revenue to meet operating expenses, including repayment of the power investment through an amortization schedule."

In 1946, BPA established annual repayment schedules for its projects, after which it eliminated progress reporting altogether.

Major Policy Changes

An economic crisis hit BPA during the late 1950s and early 1960s, causing it to depart from what it previously considered a business-like approach to repayment. A $70 million cumulative repayment surplus that had been achieved through FY 1957 was now fast approaching a cumulative repayment deficit because BPA could not meet its scheduled annual repayment requirements.

> Believing that a rate increase (Bonneville's first since 1939) would seriously impair the region's growth and should be avoided if at all possible, the administrator chose to study other alternatives.

---

[1]The Federal Columbia River Power System is the formal name of the electric generating and distribution system administered by BPA.

In 1962, he concluded that "basically, there are three ways to attack this problem: modify our financial practices and payout schedules, sell power now being wasted, and raise our rates."

In FY 1964, BPA eliminated scheduled annual repayments and adopted a revised policy of forecasting future revenues—the repayment method:

> Under this method, estimated revenues are projected to cover projected expenses, including the federal investment over the repayment period of the facility. The repayment is designed to demonstrate revenue adequacy by showing the recovery of annual costs each year and by producing a schedule of amortization payments governed by the policy of repaying federal investments within 50 years.
>
> Annual revenues are applied to pay for the costs of operation and maintenance, purchased and exchanged power, transmission, service, and amortization of the federal investment. If revenues in a single year are insufficient to repay the federal investment, the unpaid balance is then included in the total outstanding investment to be amortized over the remaining life of the project.
>
> The administrator at the time said that the change would level out year-to-year revenue fluctuations and provide rate stability over extended periods. The move to the new system had the perceived advantage of reducing a possible 30 percent increase to 2.4 percent [the larger increase would have been occasioned, presumably, had orthodox amortization procedures been followed]. [General Accounting Office 1983, pp. 2, 3][2]

This system of repayment, with minor variations, has remained the announced policy of BPA. However, the actual repayment activity has differed rather markedly from the announced one.

Repayment Practices since the 1960s

BPA's actual repayments have not matched its repayment promises for about two decades. The nonpayment, in whole or in part, during such an extended period suggests rather strongly that subsidization is taking place. A total failure to repay would convert the funds advanced or borrowed by BPA to explicit subsidies. The postponement of repayment does not, in and of itself, constitute a subsidy equal to the amount of the principal that is not repaid.

---

[2]The rate increase refers to increases in the electric rates in the region.

Delayed repayment does constitute subsidization to the extent of the unpaid interest accruing on the delayed repayments. This would be a relatively minor item, however, if the delayed repayments were made in timely fashion with full payment of interest.

In the case of BPA, nonpayment rather than payment has been the rule rather than the exception. Beginning in FY 1973, the repayment percentage of outstanding investment fell steadily. See Table 3.1, which presents the history of BPA's operating profits and losses and the ratios of repayment to total investment. For example, the ratio of cumulative repayment to federal investment was 19 percent in FY 1972 but kept falling until it reached slightly over 8.3 percent in FY 1983 and then rose to 11.6 percent in FY 1986. BPA estimated that the ratio would go still higher in FY 1987, to over 13 percent, but that may be overly optimistic.

This performance by BPA has drawn sharp criticism from both GAO and OMB. When David Stockman, then OMB director, testified before a congressional committee in 1985, he was very critical of BPA. For example, he asserted that BPA is the beneficiary of an indefinite deferrable payment (IDP) mortgage with respect to its debt to the U.S. Treasury. Stockman noted that

> Any slight change in Bonneville's business plans—either cost increases or revenue shortfalls—results in a deferral of planned debt repayment. Under the IDP mortgage concept, any deferred payment is simply rescheduled to be repaid in future years—so long as the 50 year project by project "balloon payment dates" are met. . . . Consequently, each and every repayment study shows that Bonneville is "on schedule" in repaying its debt—*even when they actually repay nothing* [emphasis in original]. [Office of Management and Budget 1985, p. 12]

Stockman emphasized his point by comparing BPA's actual payments with those promised in its published repayment studies. His comparisons were drawn from selected repayment studies from FY 1977 to FY 1984. The shortfalls between promised and actual payments in the selected years ranged from $401 million to $1.02 billion. I followed Stockman's methodology, but I filled in the years he omitted and included actual repayments through FY 1986. These results are presented in Table 3.2. These repayments are subtracted from the projected repayments during the periods covered. These differences, called shortfalls, are given as totals but are also averaged over the periods in question. Comparing the projections made

Table 3.1

BPA's OPERATING AND REPAYMENT HISTORY

Fiscal Year	Net Operating Income (or Loss) ($ Thousands)	Cumulative Plant in Service ($ Thousands)	Repayment Annual ($ Thousands)	Repayment Cumulative ($ Thousands)	Unpaid Balance ($ Thousands)	Repayment as % of Investment
1939–65	202,791	1,802,230	363,694	363,694	—	20.2
1966–72	151,364	3,131,054	231,313	595,007	—	19.0
1973	(24,055)	3,563,570	1,424	596,431	2,967,139	16.7
1974	(37,859)	3,680,337	0	596,431	3,083,906	16.2
1975	22,318	4,007,868	21,875	618,306	3,389,562	15.4
1976	67,126	4,705,129	3,347	621,653	4,083,476	13.2
1977	(49,333)	5,114,022	6,807	628,460	4,485,562	12.3
1978	(17,064)	5,533,230	7,131	635,591	4,897,639	11.5
1979	(69,949)	5,754,800	940	636,531	5,118,269	11.1
1980	(59,490)	6,009,790	75	636,606	5,373,184	10.6
1981	(5,891)	6,432,585	1,703	638,309	5,794,276	9.9
1982	(129,456)	7,030,110	0	638,309	6,391,801	9.1
1983	14,038	7,630,703	0	638,309	6,992,394	8.4
1984	101,030	8,227,517	1,321	638,309	7,587,827	7.8
1985	223,448	8,622,486	227,816	867,506	7,754,981	10.0
1986	(64,916)	9,114,920	190,800	1,058,305	8,056,615	11.6

NOTE: I find that the BPA figures are extremely difficult to reconcile. The 1984 and 1985 repayment studies, for example, show an unpaid balance of about $7.6 billion. In 1984, however, a report to Congress states that the unpaid balance was $8 billion at the end of 1984. I have used the lower figure to give a conservative estimate of the ratio.

SOURCES: General Accounting Office 1983, p. 5; U.S. Department of Energy, Bonneville Power Administration 1985a (pp. 30, 31, 34); 1985b (pp. 60, 61); 1986a (p. 35); 1987 (p. 37).

Table 3.2
DIFFERENCES BETWEEN BPA PROJECTED AND ACTUAL PAYMENTS, 1977–86 ($ MILLIONS)

Projected Payments, 1978–1986
According to BPA Repayment Studies of Given Years

Fiscal Years	1977	1978	1979	1980	1981	1982	1983	1984	Actual Payments (Rounded)
1978	55								7
1979	33	94							1
1980	59	77	118						0
1981	116	116	78	180					2
1982	141	189	96	267	197				0
1983	139	218	113	270	163	6			0
1984	146	231	83	305	182	181	0		0
1985	153	235	102	285	110	197	247	247	237
1986	155	234	134	297	119	104	92	92	191
Total Projected Payments	997	1,394	724	1,604	771	488	339	339	439

Repayments for Years Covered[a]							
438	431	430	430	428	428	428	428
Shortfalls							
559	963	294	1,174	343	60	(89)	(89)
			(Average Shortfall = 402)				
Average Shortfall per Year							
62	120	42	196	69	15	(30)	(44)
		(Average of Averages = 54)					

[a]The figures in this row give the actual repayments for the years projected for example, in the 1977 column, the repayments are those projected by BPA for the fiscal years 1978 to 1986.

SOURCES: U.S. Department of Energy, Bonneville Power Administration 1978 (pp. 24, 25); 1979a (pp. 38, 39); 1979b (pp. 40, 41); 1981 (pp. 58, 59); 1983 (pp. 48, 49); 1984 (pp. 32, 33); 1985a (pp. 30, 31); 1986; 1987 (p. 3); Office of Management and Budget 1985, p. 13.

in the annual reports from 1978 to 1982, we see that the differences between projected and actual payments (shortfalls) ranged from $60 million to $1.17 billion. These differences averaged between $15 million and $196 million per year for the years of shortfall. The actual repayments did exceed the projected payments for FY 1985 and FY 1986 of the 1983 and 1984 annual reports.

Two comments are in order regarding BPA's increases in its repayments in FY 1985 and FY 1986. First, these increases may have been in response to criticisms from the Office of Management and Budget (OMB) and from other sources. Second, the modest excesses of repayments over the last two projections ($89 million) per year do not come close to making up the shortfalls of the previous repayment projections.

Sound business principles, of course, call for regular amortization, usually on a straight-line basis (as exemplified by an ordinary household mortgage). Indeed, BPA promised such an amortization procedure early in its history, as noted above. Stockman estimates the differences beween BPA's repayments from FY 1975 to FY 1984 and the repayments that would have made according to a straight-line amortization of 2 percent per year (Table 3.3). That is as if BPA had complied with its legal mandate to retire its debt on all projects within 50 years.

I revised and expanded this effort, with the results being shown in Table 3.4. I took into account the increments to BPA's system and calculated what the amortization would be on straight-line amortization of 2 percent per year on the entire investment. This is shown as "required payment" in the table. The actual payments are compared and differences are termed shortfalls. The cumulative shortfall estimated from these data amounts to about $1.05 billion. Stockman argued that based on his data "of all lenders, only the deficit-ridden Federal taxpayer lends money with IDP mortgages." He noted further that "if IDP mortgages are not stopped, future deficits could be even more adversely impacted" (Office of Management and Budget 1985, p. 16). The results of Table 3.4 reinforce this conclusion. The precise percentage of these deferred payments that amount to subsidy is open to question. But there is substantial subsidization, and the American taxpayers feel the adverse effects noted by Stockman.

I estimated shortfalls in BPA amortizations in a slightly different way. They were measured by the failure to keep cumulative repayment up to a given percentage of government investment. Table 3.5

Table 3.3

BPA's Total Debt-Repayment Shortfall, 1974–84 ($ Millions)

Differences between Total Debt Repayment and Normal Amortization Repayment

	Typical Amortization Schedule*	BPA Actual Amortization	Annual Shortfall	Cumulative Shortfall
FY 1974 Unpaid Debt	3,658	3,658	3,658	3,658
Annual Repayment of 1974 Unpaid Debt				
FY 1975	73	22	51	51
FY 1976	73	3	70	121
FY 1977	73	7	66	187
FY 1978	73	7	66	253
FY 1979	73	1	72	325
FY 1980	73	0	73	398
FY 1981	73	2	71	469
FY 1982	73	0	73	542
FY 1983	73	0	73	615
FY 1984	73	0	73	688
Total	730	42	688	688

*Assumes repayment on a straight-line basis over 50 years, that is, 2 percent amortization per year. This is actually understated because it assumes that all of BPA's 1974 unpaid debt of about $3.6 billion is amortized over 50 years, when in fact much of that debt has been on BPA's books for some time and should be amortized much faster.

Source: Office of Management and Budget 1985, p. 11.

Table 3.4
BPA's Total Debt Repayment, Including Increments, 1973–86 ($ Thousands)

Compared to Normal Amortization Repayments

Fiscal Year	Cumulative Unpaid Balance	Increment	2% Amortization (Incremental)	Required Payment	Actual Payment	Annual Shortfall	Cumulative Shortfall
1973	2,967,139	—	59,343	59,343	1,424	57,919	57,919
1974	3,083,906	116,767	2,335	61,678	0	61,678	119,597
1975	3,389,562	305,656	6,113	67,791	21,875	45,916	165,513
1976	4,083,476	693,914	13,876	81,667	3,347	78,320	243,833
1977	4,485,562	402,086	8,042	89,709	6,807	82,902	326,735
1978	4,897,639	412,077	8,242	97,951	7,131	90,820	417,555
1979	5,118,269	220,630	4,413	102,364	940	101,424	518,979
1980	5,373,184	254,915	5,098	107,462	75	107,387	626,366
1981	5,794,276	421,092	8,422	115,884	1,703	114,811	741,177
1982	6,391,801	597,525	11,950	127,834	0	127,834	869,011
1983	6,992,394	600,593	12,012	139,846	0	139,846	1,008,857
1984	7,587,888	595,494	11,910	151,756	1,321	150,435	1,159,292
1985	7,745,857	157,969	3,159	154,915	237,000	(82,085)	1,077,207
1986	8,047,491	301,634	6,033	160,948	190,800	(29,852)	1,047,355

SOURCES: General Accounting Office 1981, p. 6; U.S. Departments of Energy and Interior 1975, 1977 through 1980. (Calculated from various tables in these reports.)

Table 3.5

BPA's ACTUAL REPAYMENTS COMPARED TO HYPOTHETICAL REPAYMENTS AT VARIOUS PERCENTAGES OF INVESTMENT, 1973–86 ($ THOUSANDS)

Fiscal Year	Value of Cumulative Plant in Service	Cumulative Repayment at 13%	Cumulative Repayment at 12%	Actual Cumulative Repayment	Differences at 13%	Differences at 12%
1973	3,563,570	463,264	427,628	595,007	131,743	167,379
1974	3,680,337	478,444	441,640	596,431	117,987	154,791
1975	4,007,868	521,023	480,944	618,306	97,283	137,362
1976	4,705,129	611,667	564,615	621,653	9,986	57,038
1977	5,114,022	664,823	613,683	628,460	(36,363)	(14,777)
1978	5,533,230	719,320	663,988	635,591	(83,729)	(28,397)
1979	5,754,800	748,124	690,576	636,531	(111,593)	(54,045)
1980	6,009,790	781,273	721,175	636,606	(144,667)	(84,569)
1981	6,432,585	836,236	771,910	638,309	(197,927)	(133,601)
1982	7,030,110	913,914	843,613	638,309	(275,605)	(205,304)
1983	7,630,703	991,991	915,684	638,309	(353,682)	(277,315)
1984	8,227,517	1,069,577	987,302	639,690	(429,887)	(347,612)
1985	8,622,486	1,120,923	1,034,698	876,690	(244,233)	(158,008)
1986	9,114,920	1,184,940	1,093,790	1,067,490	(117,450)	(26,300)
Totals					(1,638,137)	(783,804)

SOURCES: General Accounting Office 1981; U.S. Departments of Energy and Interior (1975 through 1986).

traces through the effects of maintaining this percentage at 13 percent. This was the percentage achieved in 1975 and bears some relationship to that discussed in a Reagan administration proposal to sell BPA to private interests (as discussed later in this chapter). The table also traces the effects of maintaining the percentage at 12 percent.

Had the percentages been maintained at 12 percent or 13 percent, BPA would have made additional payments amounting to about $784 million or $1.63 billion, respectively (figures rounded from table).

These figures are rather consistent with the estimates obtained by a conventional amortization schedule. The insistence on maintaining a fixed ratio of cumulative amortization to investment may appear to be somewhat mechanistic. But it does help to take into account new investment in the amortization ratios. It gives at least an estimate of whether new investments are being amortized at the same rate as previous investments.

Interest-Rate Subsidies

BPA's interest-rate policy has drawn strong criticism from both GAO and OMB. These agencies agree that Pacific Northwest electric ratepayers have been the beneficiaries of significant subsidies from the general taxpayers because of the low interest rates paid by BPA. The rates paid by BPA have been below not only market rates but even Treasury borrowing rates.

The interest rates paid by BPA on its long-term borrowings from the U.S. Treasury bear a regular relationship to government borrowing rates. Under the Federal Columbia River Transmission System Act of 1974, the interest on BPA's long-term debt is set at rates comparable to debt issued by U.S. government corporations. BPA's annual report for 1986 states that the weighted average interest rate paid on its borrowings was 11 percent and 12.3 percent as of September 30, 1986, and September 30, 1985, respectively (U.S. Departments of Energy and Interior 1986, p. 43).

The rates paid on appropriated funds are much lower, as BPA notes in its annual report. "Interest rates on the appropriated funds range from 2.5% to 12.4% (the weighted average rate was 3.5% in 1966 and 3.2% in 1985). These rates have been set by law, administrative order pursuant to law, or administrative policies." Earlier annual reports completed the thought in saying, "and have not necessarily been established to recover the interest costs to the U.S.

Treasury to finance the investment" (U.S. Department of Energy, Bonneville Power Administration 1987, p. 44).

In testimony before a congressional committee, David Stockman, OMB director in the early years of the Reagan administration, offered rather sharp and incisive comments about the subsidization involved in the rates set by BPA. He pointed out that the original practices of BPA (and the other power-marketing administrations) did employ interest rates that were tied to Treasury borrowings, which of course were below private market rates. He noted that practices in recent years resulted in a continuing erosion of the cost-recovery principle. Throughout the 1940s and into the 1950s the Corps of Engineers and the Bureau of Reclamation continued to use interest rates on borrowings of 2.5 percent and a maximum of 3.0 percent, respectively, although Treasury long-term borrowing rates were rising into the 3–4 percent range.[3] Even a 1970 directive by the Department of Interior resulted in a 1970 interest rate that was 2.5 percent below contemporary Treasury borrowing costs—4.85 percent versus 7.35 percent, although it did make some improvements. In addition, two provisions in this directive tended to perpetuate at least some subsidization. First, future-year adjustments were capped at 0.5 percent per year, virtually ensuring that future-year repayment rates would never catch up to Treasury rates that were rising. Second, and most important, all ongoing projects—even though authorized but not yet constructed—were grandfathered (Office of Management and Budget 1985, pp. 4–5).

These practices have resulted in BPA's rates lying below Treasury borrowing rates since the 1950s. Figure 3.1 displays the differences between BPA rates and Treasury rates and the differences between BPA's rates and market rates. In his testimony, Stockman followed up with estimates of the interest subsidies involved in only six of BPA's projects, as presented in Table 3.6. He also pointed out that project additions and improvements to existing projects were financed under the old repayment rules, thereby completely circumventing what little cost-recovery protection otherwise existed. Stockman's estimates of the subsidies for five of the additions and improvements to the BPA system are presented in Table 3.7. The estimated

[3]The interest rates on some Bureau of Reclamation projects are set by statute, as for example, the third powerhouse at Grand Coulee Dam. Stockman complained that the exception of setting interest rates by statute was larger than the rule (Office of Management and Budget 1985, p. 4).

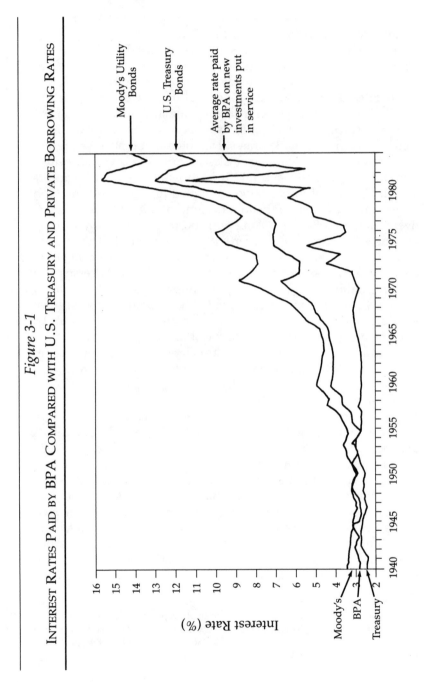

Figure 3-1

INTEREST RATES PAID BY BPA COMPARED WITH U.S. TREASURY AND PRIVATE BORROWING RATES

Table 3.6
EFFECTS OF DIFFERENCES BETWEEN TREASURY BORROWING RATES AND BPA BORROWING RATES ON SELECTED BPA PROJECTS

	Project			Interest-Rate Subsidy			
Project	Project Cost[a] ($ millions)	Project Construction Period	Repayment Interest Rate (%)	Actual Treasury Cost of Borrowing[b] (%)	Subsidy (%)	Estimated Subsidy[c] ($ millions)
McNary	$276	1949–1960	2.5%	2.63%	0.13%	$8
Dworshak	$297	1962–1973	2.625%	6.22%	3.595%	$150
John Day	$393	1959–1972	2.5%	4.78%	2.28%	$137
Libby	$421	1966–1976	3.125%	6.57%	3.445%	$186
Lower Granite	$268	1965–1975	2.5%	6.79%	4.29%	$141
Lower Monumental	$149	1961–1970	2.5%	4.98%	2.48%	$49
Total						$671

[a]Allocation to power only.

[b]Weighted average Treasury long-term rate for the years in which the project was constructed.

[c]Computed on a present value basis over a 50-year period from the project in-service date.

NOTE: The estimated subsidies are calculated as the present values of the differences between Treasury borrowing rates and BPA borrowing rates over the life of its project. The same is true in Table 3.7.

SOURCE: Office of Management and Budget 1985, p.6.

Table 3.7

EFFECTS OF DIFFERENCES BETWEEN TREASURY BORROWING RATES AND BPA BORROWING RATES ON SELECTED ADDITIONS AND IMPROVEMENTS TO BPA PROJECTS

Original Project		Project Additions and Improvements			Interest Rate Subsidy			
Completed Cost[a] (\$M)	In-Service	Completed Cost[a] (\$M)	In-Service	Years between Completions	Repayment Interest Rate (%)	Treasury Borrowing Cost[b] (%)	Interest Rate Subsidy (%)	Estimated Subsidy[c] (\$ Millions)
Bonneville								
Dam	65	1944	639	1983	39	3.25	10.4	7.15	409
Chief Joseph	146	1958	333	1979	21	3.25	8.2	4.95	173
Grand Coulee	213	1951	587	1980	29	3.25	7.3	4.05	207
The Dalles	225	1961	55	1974	13	3.125	6.5	3.375	24
Ice Harbor	95	1962	39	1976	14	3.25	7.7	4.45	22
Total	744		1,653						835

[a]Allocation to power only.
[b]Weighted average Treasury long-term rate for the project construction period.
[c]Computed on a present value basis over a 50-year period from the project in-service date.

SOURCE: Office of Management and Budget 1985, p. 8.

subsidies are calculated as the present values of the differences between Treasury borrowing rates and BPA borrowing rates over the life of the project.

In criticizing BPA's interest-rate policies, GAO noted that the annual interest costs during the construction of projects are not repaid but instead are capitalized. That is, the interest is accrued during the interest period and added to the other construction costs. GAO complained that the interest rates for project construction funds have been set at levels below Treasury borrowing rates. BPA also used a single interest rate established at the start of the project for computing interest for both the construction period and the repayment period.

The GAO report states: "The financing for construction of Bonneville Dam's second powerhouse illustrates the two interest rate practices of BPA. This major addition to the Bonneville project built from 1967 through 1985, at a cost of about $625 million, was assigned an interest rate of 3.25 percent, which remained fixed the entire 19-year construction period. During this time the Treasury borrowing rate ranged from a low of 4.85 percent to a high of 12.87 percent in 1981" (General Accounting Office 1986, pp. 11–12). GAO estimated the effects of these low interest rates in comparison with Treasury borrowing rates, as shown in Table 3.8.

The table shows the effects of using the BPA interest rate and two alternatives during the repayment period of 50 years. The BPA method uses a rate of 3.25 percent. Alternative 1 uses a composite rate based on Treasury rates in effect during construction. In this case, the estimated rate is 9.47 percent, or a 191 percent increase over the BPA method. Alternative 2 combines the use of the composite rate with the use of compound interest rather than simple interest during construction. The present value of future interest expense under the two alternatives is calculated using a discount rate of 10.75 percent, which was the 1985 Treasury long-term borrowing rate. The present values of future interest payments in excess of agency payments are $353.4 million and $449.2 million under alternatives 1 and 2, respectively.

I have made an additional attempt to estimate the effects of the use of interest rates by BPA that were below both Treasury borrowing rates and private market rates. Table 3.9 presents my estimates of the implicit subsidies to BPA stemming from the use of sub-Treasury and sub-market rates from FY 1976 to FY 1984. Estimates of new BPA investments put in service each year, as given in column

Table 3.8

COMPARISON BETWEEN BPA METHOD AND GAO ALTERNATIVES
FOR COMPUTING INTEREST DURING 50-YEAR REPAYMENT
PERIOD FOR SECOND POWERHOUSE AT BONNEVILLE DAM

	Total federal investment (principal)	Repayment interest rate	1985 annual interest expense	Present value (1985) of total future interest expense
	—— (dollars are in millions) ——			
Agency method	$622.9	3.25%	$19.9	$184.4
Alternative 1	$622.9	9.47%	$59.0	$537.9
Increase over BPA method		6.22%	$39.1	$353.4
Percentage change		191%	196%	192%
Alternative 2	$734.1	9.47%	$96.5	$633.6
Increase over BPA method	$111.2	6.22%	$49.6	$449.2
Percentage change	18%	191%	249%	244%

SOURCE: General Accounting Office 1986, p. 18.
NOTE: Alternative 1 uses a composite rate based on Treasury rates in effect during construction. Alternative 2 combines the use of the composite rate with the use of compound interest during construction.

2, were derived from the agency's annual reports. The difference during this period between the average rates paid on new investments and Treasury rates is given in column 3, and the deficit (difference in interest rates multiplied by number of new investments) is given in column 4. Columns 5 and 6 repeat the procedure with respect to market rates that are approximated by the rates on Moody's utility bonds. The implicit subsidy effects in terms of Treasury rates and market rates amount to $97.3 million and $144.6 million, respectively.

Table 3.10 combines the results of Tables 3.4 and 3.9 and estimates the shortfalls of a mortgage-like arrangement whereby 2 percent of the increment is paid along with interest at Treasury borrowing rates. (This table also gives the greater shortfalls with market rates.)

Table 3.9

ESTIMATED EFFECTS ON BPA's BORROWING COSTS OF SUB-TREASURY AND SUB-MARKET RATES, 1976–84

Fiscal Year	New Investment (excluding Transmission System) ($ Thousands)	Difference between BPA and Treasury Rates (%)	Implicit Subsidies ($ Thousands)***	Difference between BPA and Market Rates (%)*	Implicit Subsidies ($ Thousands)***
1976	402,466**	3.48	14,006	5.62	22,619
1977	402,466**	3.06	12,315	4.43	17,829
1978	328,547	2.79	9,166	4.0	13,142
1979	153,518	2.64	4,053	4.12	6,325
1980	206,935	5.71	11,816	8.12	16,803
1981	148,492	1.67	2,480	4.1	6,088
1982	523,874	7.03	36,828	9.59	50,240
1983	184,667	2.84	5,244	4.83	8,919
1984	63,226	2.19	1,385	4.21	2,662
Totals			97,293		144,627

*Measured by Moody's utility bond rates.

**Estimated on a straight-line basis of the aggregate investment of 1976 and 1977.

***Implicit subsidy equals amount of new investment multiplied by the differences in the rates noted.

SOURCES: Calculated from data in U.S. Departments of Energy and Interior (1976 through 1984); Office of Management and Budget 1985.

Table 3.10

SUMMARY OF ESTIMATED EFFECTS OF STRAIGHT-LINE AMORTIZATION AT TREASURY AND MARKET RATES, 1976–84

Fiscal Year	Principal Shortfall ($ Thousands)[a]	Interest Shortfall ($ Thousands)[b] Treasury Rates	Sum of Shortfalls ($ Thousands)	Revenue from Power Sales ($ Thousands)	Required Payment ($ Thousands)[c]	Percentage Shortfall[d]
1976	78,320	14,006	92,326	271,045	363,371	34
1977	82,903	12,315	95,218	194,605	289,823	49
1978	90,820	9,166	99,986	295,665	395,651	34
1979	101,424	4,053	105,477	257,519	362,996	41
1980	107,387	11,816	119,203	470,722	589,925	25
1981	114,811	2,480	117,291	651,079	768,370	18
1982	127,834	36,828	164,662	1,269,580	1,434,242	13
1983	139,846	5,250	145,096	1,782,339	1,927,435	8
1984	150,435	1,385	151,820	2,545,355	2,697,175	6
Total			1,091,079			25.3[e]

Table 3.10 (continued)

Fiscal Year	Principal Shortfall ($ Thousands)[a]	Interest Shortfall ($ Thousands)[b] Treasury Rates	Sum of Shortfalls ($ Thousands)	Revenue from Power Sales ($ Thousands)	Required Payment ($ Thousands)[c]	Percentage Shortfall[d]
1976	78,320	22,618	100,938	271,045	371,983	37
1977	82,903	17,829	100,732	194,605	295,337	52
1978	90,820	13,142	103,962	295,665	399,627	35
1979	101,424	6,324	107,748	257,519	365,267	42
1980	107,387	16,803	124,190	470,722	594,912	26
1981	114,811	6,088	120,899	651,079	771,978	18
1982	127,834	50,240	178,074	1,269,580	1,447,654	14
1983	139,846	8,929	148,775	1,782,339	1,931,114	8
1984	150,435	2,662	153,097	2,545,335	2,698,432	6
Total			1,138,415			26.4[d]

[a]From Table 3.4.
[b]From Table 3.9.
[c]Sum of shortfalls plus revenue from power sales.
[d]Required payment divided by revenue from power sales.
[e]Annual average percentage.

This table compares the shortfalls, at Treasury borrowing rates, with the power revenues actually received by BPA during the period from FY 1986 to FY 1984. The increases in power rates that would have been necessary to eliminate these shortfalls would be approximately 25 or 26 percent. In other words, the rates would have to be increased that much in order to bring BPA repayment in line with standard amortization practices.

Table 3.11 represents a summary of the various estimates of subsidization presented in the preceding tables. These estimates are not precise, but a fairly clear picture appears to emerge. For more than a decade, BPA has received substantial subsidies from

Table 3.11

SUMMARY OF SUBSIDY ESTIMATES

Estimate Category	Amount ($ Thousands)
Total Subsidies	
Cumulative shortfall in amortization of principal, 1973–86[a]	1,047,355
Cumulative shortfall in amortization of principal and interest (based on Treasury rates) 1976–84[b]	1,091,079
Cumulative shortfall in amortization at 13%, 1973–86[c]	1,638,137
Cumulative shortfall in amortization at 12%, 1973–86[c]	783,804
Shortfalls of principal—BPA's projections (average 1977–84)[d]	401,875
Partial Subsidies (present values)	
(original projects)[e]	671,000
(selected additions and improvements)[f]	835,000
(Bonneville Dam second powerhouse)[g]	449,000

[a]From Table 3.4.
[b]From Table 3.10.
[c]From Table 3.5.
[d]From Table 3.2.
[e]From Table 3.6.
[f]From Table 3.7.
[g]From Table 3.8.

the American taxpayer. The estimates of the total subsidies to BPA's operations from 1973 to 1986 range from about $784 million to $1.64 billion. The shortfalls from BPA's own projections of repayment of principal average about $402 million from 1977 to 1984. Subsidies to some of BPA's original projects and to selected additions and improvements to BPA's installations are estimated to range from about $450 million to about $835 million. (These latter subsidies are called partial subsidies.)

In late 1985, the Reagan administration proposed that BPA be sold to private interests by FY 1988 (see chapter 5). At the same time, the administration also made an interim proposal to bring BPA's repayment practices more in line with standard amortization practices. Under the interim proposal, the administration proposed legislation that would require BPA to adhere to a fixed 50-year amortization schedule after a project was put into service unless the useful life of the project were less. This would be a straight-line amortization of the type illustrated here. This interim proposal would increase BPA's incremental amortization of principal from $148.6 million to $304.7 million in FY 1987 (Department of Energy 1986, p. BP–8). Stockman, in his testimony, advised an incremental payment of principal and interest by BPA of $2.02 billion in the period from FY 1986 to FY 1990 (Office of Management and Budget 1985, p. 24).

Stockman also estimated the rate impacts on BPA's customers. He stated, "BPA would have to raise wholesale revenues by 20% in 1986 as result of repayment reform" (Office of Management and Budget 1985, p. 28). This figure comes rather close, incidentally, to the 25 percent increase estimated above. Stockman made a worst-case assumption whereby the entire increase is allocated to the priority customers, including residential users. In this case, residential bills might rise by about 26 percent, or $24 per month. Stockman used this figure to dramatize the subsidies that have flowed to power users in the Pacific Northwest. Table 3.12, which is derived from Stockman's testimony, shows residential electricity rates in the region compared to national average rates. From 1940 to 1980, BPA's customers paid only between 24 percent and 40 percent of the national average. Under recent repayment practice (1984–86), they have paid between 56 percent and 60 percent of the national average. Under Stockman's proposed repayment reform, given his severest assumptions, the residential customers of BPA would still be paying only 79 percent of the national average. Even

Table 3.12

BPA WHOLESALE RESIDENTIAL ELECTRICITY RATES COMPARED
TO NATIONAL AVERAGE RATES, 1940–86*

		Wholesale Rates		
		BPA Priority Firm Rate (mills/Kwhr)	National Average (mills/Kwhr)	BPA Rate as % of National Average
Category	Year			
Historic				
	1940	2.8	7.0	40
	1950	2.8	7.5	37
	1960	2.8	7.5	37
	1970	3.3	7.0	47
	1980	7.4	30.0	25
Current Services				
	1984	23.1	38.8	60
	1985	22.1	40.8	54
	1986	22.7	42.9	56
Repayment Reform**				
	1986	33.8	42.9	79

NOTES: *Wholesale residential rates are those charged by BPA to retailers
of residential power.

**Stockman's estimates given under the heading of Repayment
Reform assumes that BPA follows his recommendation that the
agency amortizes its debt according to standard amortization
practices.

SOURCE: Office of Management and Budget 1985, p. 36.

without explicit subsidies, these customers would still be getting a
bargain with federal power.

In sum, the rates of BPA have been kept at artificially low levels
by the subsidies from the federal taxpayers. Were BPA to catch up
with payments of principal and interest, the subsidies would dimin-
ish, in one sense. But, of course, the power that was used at these
lower rates is lost irrevocably. The increase in rates may choke off
some of the power now or in the future. A different type of subsi-

dization would result if BPA does bring its account into some sort of rough balance at a later time. The users of power at that time will be subsidizing the use of power earlier by making up BPA's accumulated deficiencies.

In other words, the use of power has been seriously distorted over time in an economic sense. Familiar economic principles and common sense dictate that the users of a resource should pay the true costs of the production and distribution of that resource. Where the price is less than these costs, the use of the resource will be greater than is appropriate; that is, it will be economically wasteful. This has been the case, clearly, with respect to the use of BPA power for the last decade or so.

It is worth noting that this excessive use of power was occurring during the oil "crisis" of the 1970s. This served to exacerbate that "crisis" because the use of energy in the Pacific Northwest is related to energy use elsewhere in the nation. The most direct relationship is with California users because of an intertie transmission line that transmits power to California.[4] Another possible adverse result was that this excessive use of power contributed to the grossly exaggerated forecasts of future power use in the 1970s and the unfortunate planning decisions that were predicated upon these forecasts. (Recall that the more disastrous phase of the hydrothermal program was planned during that period.)

Effects of the Hydrothermal Program

The financial legacy of the ill-fated hydrothermal program has been a substantial one. BPA payments and net-billing outlays for WNP 2 prior to December 1979 of $212.5 million were deferred and are being amortized ratably over time. Since that time, the expenses for the three net-billed plants have been treated as operating expenses and are charged to a purchase and exchange power account. Table 3.13 presents the actual and the projected expenses accruing to BPA on account of the net-billing expenses from WNP 1, 2, and 3. The totals for WNP 1 and WNP 3 are presented separately and amount to about $3.87 billion. The expenses for WNP 2 amount to about $3.67 billion. The expenses for WNP 1 and WNP 3 probably represent the costs of what may be called phantom power, as the likelihood of completing either or both of these plants is small (see next chapter for discussion of these two plants). (BPA ratepayers

---

[4]The transmission system is discussed in greater detail in Chapter 4.

Table 3.13

BPA's ACTUAL AND PROJECTED EXPENSES ARISING OUT OF
NET-BILLING OBLIGATIONS AND RESIDENTIAL POWER
EXCHANGES, 1981–91 ($ THOUSANDS)

Fiscal Year	Net-Billing Expenses WNP 1 and 3	Net-Billing Expenses WNP 2	Total	Residential Exchanges Costs
1981	99,390	106,246	205,636	
1982	213,362	168,047	381,409	216,593
1983	363,325	269,682	633,007	149,398
1984	404,680	393,169	797,849	184,296
1985	412,511	357,843	770,354	207,752
1986	375,148	375,937	751,085	208,287
1987*	403,200	381,200	784,400	
1988*	406,200	398,000	804,200	
1989*	393,500	397,100	790,600	
1990*	395,600	404,300	799,900	
1991*	401,100	420,700	821,800	
Total	3,868,016	3,672,224	7,540,240	966,326

*Projected expenses.

SOURCE: U.S. Department of Energy, Bonneville Power Administration (1981 through 1986).

will have the costs of the nonexistent power added to their electricity bills.

Another residual effect of the hydrothermal program stems from the so-called present termination commitment.[5] BPA has described this as follows:

> The Present Termination Commitment represents the outstanding debt issued to finance the projects [WNP 1, 2, and 3 and two other projects] as of September 30, 1984 (without inclusion of costs and credits which can be associated with termination of construction, salvage of assets and utilization of unspent construction funds) which would be payable over the varied financial repayment peri-

[5]BPA has presented estimates of the costs of the present termination commitment in its annual reports from at least FY 1975 through FY 1984. However, it omitted such estimates from its FY 1985 and FY 1986 reports.

ods if the projects were terminated. [The estimates for WNP 1 and 3 amount to about $3.9 billion]. [U.S. Department of Energy, Bonneville Power Administration, 1984, p. 41]

Whatever route BPA takes, preservation or abandonment, the costs that are likely to be passed on to the agency's ratepayers or the American taxpayers may be significant indeed.

Effects of the Regional Power Act

The 1980 act also left its financial legacy. The so-called residential exchanges of power for the benefit of the farm and residential customers have occasioned much litigation (see next chapter). This mechanism—which in fact involves only the exchange of paper, not power—was a device to lower the costs of the farm and residential customers of private utilities so as to defuse the customers' attacks on the then existing system. Between FY 1981 and FY 1986, the costs of the residential exchanges amounted to about $966 million (see Table 3.13).

The Regional Power Act also extended the authority of BPA to enter into billings-credits arrangements that are similar in nature to the net-billing procedures. BPA is empowered to acquire new generating facilities, including conservation installations that serve to reduce power demands. The costs of these facilities are averaged, as in net-billing, among BPA's ratepayers. In particular, BPA is empowered to finance lessened energy use by conservation and renewable resource acquisition programs. Total BPA-funded conservation amounted to $139 million in FY 1985 and was estimated to amount to $106.8 million and $117.5 million in FY 1986 and FY 1987, respectively (U.S. Department of Energy 1986, p. BP–23).

Other expenses accruing to BPA as a result of the 1980 act arise out of the preservation of the fish and wildlife resources in the area and the expenses of maintaining the Pacific Northwest Planning Council. The funded program for fish and wildlife amounted to $26 million in FY 1985 and was estimated to amount to $34 million and $44 million in FY 1986 and FY 1987, respectively (U.S. Department of Energy 1986, p. BP–49).

Possible Litigation Expenses

Although BPA appears generally confident about avoiding liability in the pending litigation arising out of the hydrothermal program (see next chapter), there are two cases that may well go against the agency.

One such case is the following, as described by BPA:

> WNP Nos. 1 and 4 and WNP Nos. 3 and 5 share certain common facilities. The participants of the terminated projects have demanded that the heretofore equitably shared costs be reallocated retro-actively to WNP Nos. 1 and 3. If the plaintiffs are successful, this could result in these two projects assuming additional costs of $192 million to $400 million. Because of the net-billing agreements discussed in Note 4, which require BPA to pay the participants' portion of the annual project costs for WNP Nos. 1, 2, and 3, BPA might be required to fund judgments against the Supply System (WPPSS) affecting the net-billed projects. BPA cannot predict the outcome of this matter. [U.S. Department of Energy 1986, p. 49]

A second case involves the attempts by creditors of WPPSS to hold BPA liable for the costs of mothballing and terminating the two nuclear plants, WNP 4 and WNP 5, that were not net-billed (see next chapter). The agency itself has stated that "BPA will vigorously oppose any attempt of these litigants to satisfy their claims from the assets of WNP Nos. 1, 2, and 3, but BPA cannot predict the outcome of these claims until they are made" (U.S. Department of Energy 1986, p. 48).

In addition, BPA could be mistaken about the outcome of other litigation. These contingent liabilities could add still more costs for BPA to amortize. Given the previous history of BPA in this regard, there is significant probability that these costs may be passed on to the American taxpayers.

Summary and Conclusion

The basic premise of public power policy throughout the United States has been that electricity can be supplied inexpensively in accordance with sound business principles. A fair interpretation of this premise is that all the costs of power generation and distribution could be recovered from the power revenues received. Covering such costs involves the timely repayment of debt obligations, which go to the Treasury in the case of BPA. The agency has long conceded this point and has pledged itself, repeatedly, to amortize its debt in a reasonably businesslike fashion.

BPA has repeatedly set up repayment schedules that promise to amortize its debt in some responsible fashion, but it has failed to implement this promise throughout its history. GAO has offered repeated criticisms of BPA's repayment policies, and OMB has offered even stronger criticisms. These agency criticisms and mine, together with the empirical evidence summarized here, controvert, rather strongly, the proposition that BPA has conducted its operations according to sound business principles.

BPA's failure to amortize its debt in a businesslike fashion implies that subsidies from the U.S. taxpayers, rather than the supposed cost advantages of public power provision, have accounted for the low prices charged for power in the Pacific Northwest. BPA would have had to raise its rates significantly to conform to an economically reasonable amortization schedule.

BPA has a significant advantage in this regard over private households and firms, which are not allowed to fall behind in the amortization of their debts, even if they keep up with the interest payments. In the case of BPA, the American taxpayers have been called upon to forgo timely repayment and thereby to subsidize the users of electric power in the Pacific Northwest.

Several estimates have been made of the subsidies that have resulted from BPA's deficiencies in repayment. The differences between repayment according to normal amortization practices and those followed by BPA are taken as estimates of the subsidies. Another estimate is the difference between Treasury and market interest rates and the rates actually paid. These figures are rather substantial; had they been eliminated, BPA would have been compelled to raise its electricity rates substantially. These estimates range from about $784 million to $1.6 billion.

The costs incurred by BPA have been augmented considerably on account of its hydrothermal program, which was intended to circumvent the difficulties in introducing new supplies of power caused by the preference provisions. To date, however, the main contribution of the program has been a large legacy of BPA debts that must be defrayed. Indeed, the magnitude of these debts cannot be ascertained at this time. The fate of two large nuclear plants begun by WPPSS still hang in the balance. The outcome of a great deal of litigation against BPA could further raise the agency's costs.

Will these additional costs be borne by the BPA power user or will they be passed on to the U.S. taxpayer? Past BPA history suggests that the latter situation is more likely. BPA has not amortized its debt in accordance with "sound business principles," that is, according to normal amortization practices. Only if it were to do so would the continuing subsidies to the agency's operations be ended. The historical evidence suggests that only a basic change in national policy holds promise of altering BPA's repayment policies and of ending the continuing subsidies to the agency's operations.

4. Legal Consequences of Public Power Policy in the Pacific Northwest

The public power policy implemented in the Pacific Northwest has bequeathed a rich legacy of litigation to the region. Both phases of the hydrothermal program generated litigation that is still in progress. The more protracted litigation arose out of the default on the $2.25 billion owed on bonds used to finance the two aborted nuclear plants of phase 2, WNP 4 and 5. Postponement of the two nuclear plants WNP 1 and 3, which were begun under phase 1, has also provoked legal controversy. The Bonneville Power Administration is involved in litigation concerning both phase 1 and phase 2.

The Regional Power Act of 1980, which was designed to end the economic and legal warfare over power in the region, has resulted in a new round of litigation involving BPA. One of the cases arising out of the act has been ruled on by the U.S. Supreme Court, and others have been ruled on by lower courts. This litigation was added to that arising out of phase 1 and phase 2 in the 1980s.

Phase 2 of the Hydrothermal Program

On January 22, 1982, the directors of WPPSS decided to terminate construction of the Phase 2 WNP 4 and 5 plants. Some $2.25 billion of bonded obligations had already been incurred, however. The trustee for the bondholders that had supplied the funds for these plants, the Chemical Bank of New York, filed suits in Idaho, Oregon, and Washington to compel the participants in the projects to make their shares of the principal and interest payments to WPPSS, the nominal obligor on the bonds. Were the bank to prevail, the participating utilities and municipalities would be forced to raise the rates to their electricity users in order to pay for the "phantom power" from the terminated plants. The participants offered legal defenses to avoid liability. They were successful in Idaho and Washington but not in Oregon.[1] The Washington case was of particular importance because about 75 percent of the power from the two plants had been contracted to utilities and municipalities in that state. On June 15, 1983, the Washington State Supreme Court absolved the Washington PUDs, cities, and towns from liability on these obligations in one of the Chemical Bank cases. (*Chemical Bank v. Washington Public Power Supply System* 1983). The case, incidentally, sent shock waves through both the legal and financial communities.

The successful defense by the participating utilities in Washington invoked the legal doctrine of ultra vires, which in nonlegal terms means that the districts and municipalities, as corporations, did not have legal authority to enter into particular contracts. Individuals may enter into any contract that is not barred by law. Private and public corporations, however, may only enter into contracts that carry out the purposes for which they were chartered. In other words, their charters limit the kinds of obligations they may undertake by contract. Obligations that are outside of these limits are ultra vires, or "beyond the powers." Such contracts are, by law, unenforceable.

The participants conceded in court that they had the authority to contract for the delivery of electric power. But they argued that they did not have the authority to contract for the construction of plants from which power would not be delivered. Their contracts, however, clearly spelled out such obligations. The contracts were of the so-called take-or-pay variety, known more colloquially as hell-or-high-water contracts. In law, this is known as contracting for dry-hole capacity, using an analogy based on the field of oil exploration (the obligation to pay in such instances does not depend on the discovery of oil). The participants argued that the contract for dry-hole capacity was ultra vires.

The popularly elected Washington State Supreme Court sustained this defense by a margin of 7 to 2. Political passions in the Pacific Northwest were inflamed over the unexpected and unfavorable turn of events regarding the WPPSS obligations. Emotions ran high particularly in Washington, where the largest number of ratepayers was affected. It is difficult to explain the Washington court's decision on other than political grounds. Legal scholars quickly registered their disapproval in at least four law review

---

[1]Lower-court decisions were reversed on appeal in Oregon and Washington, but the net result is as stated.

articles, including two published in Washington (Degginger 1984; Shattuck 1984; Tamietti 1984; Wohabe 1984). The writers of these articles appeared to agree that the decision was a wrongful application of the ultra vires doctrine.

The arguments of these writers found great support in a very strong dissenting opinion by a 14-year veteran of the court, Justice Robert F. Utter. Some of his arguments were as follows:

> In return for consideration in the form of revenue bonds, the participants received not guaranteed power but an exclusive right to power which might or might not materialize. . . . The purchase of a possibility of power in the present case no doubt seemed equally advisable in 1974 when steadily rising energy prices were predicted and the costs of the proposed plant seemed manageable. [*Chemical Bank* 1983, p. 811]

Justice Utter went on to point out that other courts had allowed other public bodies such as municipalities (presumably with similar charters) to enter into similar contracts. He concluded that "municipalities exercising their authority to provide electric power to their citizens must be given the freedom and flexibility to use all advisable means" (*Chemical Bank* 1983, p. 813).

Another line of argument noted by the dissenting justice was the acquiescence of the state legislature in the well-publicized contractual arrangements of WPPSS, itself a creature of the legislature, and that body had not acted to clarify the law or otherwise indicate that WPPSS could not enter into such contractual arrangements. Justice Utter took this lack of action as indicative of legislative acquiescence in this matter.

Another point revolves around the legal doctrine of unjust enrichment. The law attempts to prevent contractors from using legal technicalities to escape paying for value received despite some legal flaws in a contract. Justice Utter argued that the contracts in question were analogous to option contracts. In effect, the utilities received the possibility of receiving power without paying for the right if the contracts were invalidated. These optionlike rights of value were received without recompense under the majority decision.

The remaining utilities involved in the agreements were also relieved from liability in another Washington State Supreme Court decision of the following year. The majority decision ruled that the release of some of the participants in the previous decision (whose obligations amounted to about 70 percent of the total power share) resulted in the contractual release of the remaining participants. Justice Utter, once again, presented a cogent and well-reasoned dissent and even cited the law review articles noted above (*Chemical Bank* v. *Washington Public Power Supply System* 1984).

The supreme court decisions in Washington appear to be final. The plaintiff bank was apparently unable to raise the requisite federal question to have the U.S. Supreme Court review the cases (*Chemical Bank* 1985a, 1985b). The bondholders are still pursuing remedies against WPPSS and the participating utilities. For example, a trial involving two sets of cases is scheduled to begin in federal court in Tucson, Arizona, in September 1988. (Predictions are that the trial may last as long as two years.) One set of cases involves actions by the bondholders for recovery of the bonds' face value. The other set was brought as class actions for fraud.

Attempts are ongoing to achieve a settlement between the litigants in order to prevent a long and costly trial of the issues involved.

BPA and Phase 2

There have also been attempts to involve BPA in the litigation over phase 2 since judgments against the federal agency could be collected more easily than judgments against other defendants. Chemical Bank attempted to recover damages from BPA in federal court. The bank claimed that the agency had negligently prepared electric power forecasts that were used by WPPSS in its planning for the five nuclear plants. The case against BPA was dismissed on the grounds of government immunity. Government immunity is a legal defense that is derived from the common-law notion that the king can do no wrong.

Other litigation that attempts to draw BPA into liability for the obligations of WNP 4 and 5 is now in progress. The agency has been sued for claims arising out of the WPPSS default on these plants and the delayed construction of WNP 1 and 3. In the BPA annual report for 1986, it is stated that "in the opinion of BPA General Counsel, BPA has valid defenses to the direct claims against BPA and the possibility of plaintiffs prevailing against BPA is remote" (U.S. Department of Energy, Bonneville Power Administration 1987, p. 48).

The BPA's general counsel was less sanguine about the outcome of other actions that attempt to bring BPA into the phase 2 litigation:

> In addition to direct claims against BPA, there are lawsuits against the Supply System [WPPSS] brought by the bondholders and

bond fund trustee, by utilities who loaned money to the Supply System to pay for mothballing and termination of WNP 4 and 5, and by contractors regarding claims for goods and services provided for WNP 4 and 5. Many of these litigants have asserted a right to execute on all of the assets of the Supply System including WNP Nos. 1, 2 and 3 to satisfy judgments in their favor. . . . BPA will vigorously oppose any attempts to satisfy their claims from the assets of WNP Nos. 1, 2 and 3, but BPA General Counsel cannot predict the outcome of these claims until they are made. [U.S. Department of Energy, Bonneville Power Administration 1987, p. 48]

These attempts to involve WNP 1, 2, and 3 in litigation regarding phase 2 hold serious financial peril for BPA. For one thing, these plants come under net-billing, and BPA must absorb their costs and pass them on to its ratepayers. For another, WNP 2 is now in commercial operation and producing revenues. Levying on the assets of this plant could increase BPA's cost exposure arising out of phase 1.

Another type of commingling of the assets of the two phases is now being attempted in litigation. The two plants of phase 2 were planned as twins of two of the phase 1 plants. That is, WNP 1 and 4 share joint facilities, as do WNP 3 and 5. An allocation of costs, which BPA terms "equitable," was made when these facilities were planned. The participants in the terminated WNP 4 and 5 have demanded in court that the shared costs be reallocated retroactively to WNP 1 and 3. BPA would be liable, under net-billing, for additional costs of from $192 million to $400 million. According to the 1986 BPA annual report, "BPA General Counsel cannot predict the outcome of this matter" (U.S. Department of Energy, Bonneville Power Administration 1987, p. 49).

Phase 2 of the hydrothermal program has passed into history, but its troublesome legal legacy lingers on. The only safe prediction is that much time will elapse before the various legal controversies are resolved. Indeed, a recent book on the matter concluded:

In other words, what many bondholders do not understand is that, although a settlement is possible, it is likely to result only from a protracted struggle, a legal and political war of attrition that by the end of 1985 was not even half over, even though over $100 million had already been spent on lawsuits by the many different legal combatants. And even if a settlement is reached, it may involve only a fraction of the money owed to bondholders, or a long payout period extending over many years. [Leighland and Lamb 1986, p. 229]

Phase 1 of the Hydrothermal Program

The ultra vires defense to the participants' obligations was also interposed in litigation involving WNP 1, 2, and 3. The city of Springfield, Oregon, sought to clarify its contractual rights regarding its agreement to participate in the construction of these plants.[2] The U.S. Court of Appeals for the Ninth Circuit refused, however, to invalidate the contracts for WNP 1, 2, and 3 (*City of Springfield* 1985). The court sidestepped the ultra vires issue in its ruling, however, noting that the plants were net-billed and that the dry-hole risk had been passed on to BPA. The utilities involved in phase 1 argued, as did the utilities involved in phase 2, that they were authorized to contract for the delivery of electricity and only the dry-hole capacity was in dispute. With the risk of this capacity being transferred to BPA, held the court of appeals, the controversy disappeared.

The court's disposition of this case does not mean an end to the legal problems concerning phase 1. Only WNP 2 has been completed, as noted earlier, and the fate of WNP 1 and 3 is still uncertain. One legal controversy over WNP 3 arose some time ago. This was the only plant of the five that had ownership participation by private utilities. Four investor-owned utilities contracted for a 30 percent share of the plant's ownership. When WPPSS suspended construction, these utilities sued BPA to compel completion, which was covered by net-billing. BPA and the utilities settled the suit in 1985. According to the 1986 BPA annual report, "The guiding principle of the agreements is to put the IOU's [Investor Owned Utilities] in a position similar to what they could have expected had WNP 3 not been mothballed" (U.S. Department of Energy, Bonneville Power Administration 1987, p. 49).

The settlement agreements placed BPA in a "damned if you do, damned if you don't" position, because they had the effect of raising the cost of the power to the publicly owned utilities and the other customers of BPA. According to the 1986 BPA annual report, "The

---

[2]One intervenor in this case seeking to invalidate was Peter DeFazio, an aide to Rep. James Weaver of Oregon, a bitter opponent of WPPSS. DeFazio was also involved in the unsuccessful litigation in Oregon to invalidate the contracts for WNP 4 and 5.

settlement agreements have themselves generated a new round of litigation. In the opinion of BPA General Counsel, the likelihood that the challenges to the settlement agreements will prevent them from going into effect or that any such challenges will have any financial impact on BPA is remote" (U.S. Department of Energy, Bonneville Power Administration 1987, p. 49).

Still at issue, also, is whether the two plants (WNP 1 and 3) will be completed or terminated. BPA has issued invitations for public comment regarding the various options open to it in this regard. As was the case with WNPs 4 and 5, the termination of these plants holds open the legal possibility of the entire outstanding bonded obligation of $3.7 billion being declared immediately due and payable. BPA, in effect, would be responsible for this balance under net-billing. But without termination, BPA must continue to make payments on principal and interest on those obligations. This payment was $400 million for fiscal year 1987 alone. Escaping payment does not appear to be a viable possibility for BPA, but considering the outcome of the Chemical Bank case, such predictions are hazardous. Still, BPA concedes that the case for completion of these plants is marginal at best given the current projections of future energy demands in the region (U.S. Department of Energy 1986).

BPA may be assisted somewhat by the possibility that the U.S. Department of Energy may convert WNP 1 to the production of plutonium or tritium with some electric power being generated as a by-product. The bonds used to finance this plant, however, were revenue bonds that pledged that the revenues from this plant would be used to retire those bonds. Were the ownership or revenues of the plant to be transferred to the Department of Energy, a most embarrassing circumstance would arise. The entire indebtedness on these bonds of about $2 billion might become immediately due and payable. (At the present time, the obligations on these bonds are being retired out of the proceeds of net-billing from BPA.)

Legal Consequences of the Regional Power Act

The Pacific Northwest Electric Power and Conservation Act of 1980, commonly known as the Regional Power Act, became law in December 1980 after years of legislative wrangling. The act sought to overcome the workings of the original preference provisions of the Bonneville Project Act, which had inhibited the orderly introduction of new power supplies. The act embodied a delicately balanced compromise of the various interests in conflict. Parties that were adversely affected by the preference provisions were accorded rights that lowered the costs of existing and future power supplies. The residential and farm customers of the private utilities were granted concessions that amounted to preference rights. The industrial firms were given firm rights to BPA power for the first time. The original preference customers were nominally protected by a provision that their costs of power would be no higher than they would be in the absence of the act. The net result of the Regional Power Act was to create a new set of legal controversies in the process of resolving the old ones.

Preference Rights: The Central Lincoln Case

Some weakening of the preference provisions was required if there was to be a viable compromise of the conflicting legal and economic interests. Nonetheless, some of the first contracts awarded under the 1980 act were challenged as carrying this weakening too far. One of the preference utilities challenged contracts offered to the industrial firms as violating the preference provisions that had been retained in the act. The Central Lincoln case, embodying this controversy, reached the U.S. Supreme Court for decision (Central Lincoln was one of the preference utilities). In the words of the decision:

> Section 5(a) of the [Regional Power] Act requires all power sales under the Act to be subject to the preference and priority provisions of the [Bonneville] Project Act. Section 5(d)(1)(B) requires BPA to offer each existing DSI customer a new contract that provides "an amount of power" equivalent to that [to] which such customer was entitled under its existing 1975 contract. Section 10(c) provides that the Act does not "alter, diminish, abridge, or otherwise affect" federal laws by which the public utilities are entitled to preference. Pursuant to the Regional [Power] Act, the Administrator of BPA offered new contracts to DSI customers for the same amount of power specified by the existing 1975 contracts, but based upon his interpretation of the statute and its legislative history, concluded that terms of the power sales need not be the same as they had been under the 1975 contracts. Those contracts had provided that a portion of the power supplied to DSIs could be interrupted "at any time," thus making that portion subject to the preference provisions of the [Bonneville] Project Act and enabling preference utilities to interrupt it whenever they wanted nonfirm power. The Administrator concluded that such a provision in the new contracts would conflict with the directive of

Paragraph 5(d)(1)(A) of the Regional [Power] Act that sales to DSIs should provide a portion of the Administrator's reserves for power loads. Accordingly, the new contracts allowed power interruption only to protect BPA's firm power obligations, thus reducing the amount of nonfirm power available to preference utilities.[*Aluminum Company of America* 1984, p. 2475]

The gist of this decision is that the preference utilities had a lesser claim to BPA power than had been the case prior to the passage of the Regional Power Act. BPA would not be permitted to interrupt the supplies of power to the DSIs unless they predicted a shortage of "firm power"; that is, energy that BPA expected to produce under predictable stream-flow conditions. Previously, these supplies could be interrupted for nonfirm power, which is energy in excess of firm power. This diminution of rights was thought to be a derogation of the preference provisions of the Bonneville Project Act that were preserved, nominally, in the Regional Power Act.

The preference utilities prevailed in the federal court of appeals in San Francisco (Ninth Circuit) but the U. S. Supreme Court reversed that decision on June 5, 1984 (*Central Lincoln Peoples Utility District v. Johnson* 1982). Following up on the statement of the facts of the case quoted earlier, the court's majority decision stated "The [Bonneville] Project Act's preference provisions as incorporated in the Regional Act therefore simply do not apply to the contracts that the latter Act requires BPA to offer" (*Aluminum Company of America* 1984, pp. 2475–76).

Justice John P. Stevens filed the only dissenting opinion to the majority decision. He noted, quite clearly, that there had been weakening of the preference provisions, citing two previous cases that had interpreted those provisions: "Prior to the passage of the 1980 Act, the Ninth Circuit had construed the preference provisions to prohibit the sale of power to a private customer whenever there is a preference customer willing to buy it." The Regional Power Act did purport to preserve the preference provisions, and Justice Stevens found nothing in the statute or its legislative history to give these greater rights to the industrial firms.

Whatever the legal merits of the Supreme Court decision, it did maintain the precarious balance of economic and legal interests accomplished by the Regional Power Act by sanctioning its circumvention of the preference provisions. The decision may also have ended direct challenges on the preference issue.

Litigation Related to Exchanges of Power

An essential ingredient in the compromise on the 1980 act was the lowering of power costs to the farm and residential customers of the private utilities. Part of the controversy in the region grew out of the higher electricity rates being paid by the private utilities' customers who had threatened to avail themselves of preference rights by a legal stratagem.[4] The customers were brought into the compromise by the act's provision that they would have the rights to purchase BPA power at lower rates than previously. This lowering was to be accomplished by fictitious exchanges of power between BPA and the private utilities. According to the Department of Energy:

> *Section 5(c)* provides for power exchanges and power sales between BPA and the IOU's [investor-owned utilities] at average system cost. This is intended to provide rate relief to residential and small farm consumers of IOU's. In practice, this will benefit the affected small consumers because the IOU's average system cost will be higher than the Bonneville rate, and the difference between the two costs will be reflected in rates charged the consumers. There are a number of limitations, protections, and requirements. [U.S. Department of Energy 1981, p. 86]

In other words, there is no actual exchange of power. All that happens is that the private utilities are credited with the difference between BPA's rate and the utility's average system cost.

This lowering of cost to the private utility customers necessarily raises the power rates to BPA's other customers, since BPA must sustain increased costs. For example, assume that BPA buys power from a private utility at its average system cost of $1 per unit. BPA then exchanges an equivalent amount of power at 50 cents per unit. BPA would lose 50 cents per unit on the transaction. If, however, BPA were to buy the power at $2 per unit and exchange the power at 50 cents per unit, the loss would be $1.50 per unit.

The other side of this coin is that BPA's losses are the private

---

[4]A common example cited in the congressional hearings was the case of private utility customers in Portland, Oregon, paying much higher rates than preference customers in Vancouver, Washington. The two cities lie directly across the Columbia River from each other. (U.S. Senate 1979a).

utilities' gains. They are gaining the same amount per unit that BPA is losing.

The problem was postponed for the first five years following passage of the act. During that period, the industrial firms were required to absorb the increased costs occasioned by the exchanges. After July 1, 1985, however, an upper limit was set on the costs to be borne by the industrial firms.[5]

Litigation Related to Average System Cost.

A spate of litigation arose in regard to average system cost. Several cases challenging BPA's assessment of average system cost have been decided. In all cases, it should be noted, the industrial firms have intervened on behalf of BPA because their rates would have to be raised to cover the greater costs to BPA of the exchanges. The common denominator in the suits against BPA is the claim that the agency has underestimated average system cost. Lower assessments of these costs would work to the advantage of the industrial customers and to the disadvantage of the farm and residential customers of the private utilities.

A broad challenge to BPA's determination of average system cost was made by the public utility commissioner of Oregon and three investor-owned utilities (*Public Utility Commissioners of Oregon* 1984). Although this case was dismissed on procedural grounds, it has a very interesting aspect.[6] Affidavits were offered by the utility executives regarding statements made by Peter Johnson, the BPA administrator. The executives stated that Johnson told them that he is committed to reducing BPA's industrial rates by lowering the average system cost calculation for exchanging utilities. This would have the effect of raising the rates of the residential customers of the private utilities who are the beneficiaries of the exchange. (The numerical example above illustrates this point.)

[5]After July 1, 1985, the electricity rates charged to the DSIs were to be "equitable" in relation to the industrial rates charged by public bodies and cooperatives in the region.

[6]Several of the challenges to BPA under the Regional Power Act were dismissed for having been instituted in the wrong court—that is, on jurisdictional grounds. The act specifies that cases under the act must be brought in the U.S. Court of Appeals for the Ninth Circuit in San Francisco. For various reasons, litigants have attempted to have their cases adjudicated in the U.S. district court in Oregon, where these cases would ordinarily be adjudicated. These efforts have not been successful, in general.

Two companion cases decided by the U.S. Court of Appeals, Ninth Circuit, on July 28, 1986, revolved around a rather abrupt change in the average system cost methodology made by BPA that did have the effect noted in the affidavits. In 1981, the agency adopted a methodology that received the requisite statutory approval by the Federal Energy Regulatory Commission (FERC) in 1983. A few days after the FERC approval, however, BPA began the process of revising the methodology.

In one suit, *Pacific Power and Light* v. *Bonneville Power Administration*, some investor-owned utilities were joined by the public utility commissions of Idaho and Oregon in attacking BPA's change in methodology. The plaintiffs claimed that this change breached BPA's contractual obligations with them. This case was dismissed on jurisdictional grounds (*Pacific Power and Light* 1986).

The companion case, *Pacificorp.* v. *Federal Energy Regulatory Commission*, did involve matters of substance. Private utilities brought the case, together with state regulatory agencies. Following the pattern in these cases, a trade association representing the publicly owned utilities and the industrial firms intervened to defend BPA's calculation.

The substantive issue concerned the change in BPA methodology, which served to reduce average system cost in two ways. First, it eliminated income taxes from the calculations. Second, it eliminated return on equity as a cost factor and substituted for it the embedded cost of long-term debt. The utilities argued that the change in methodology was at variance with the legislative history of the act. They noted that Sen. James A. McClure of Idaho, one of the act's principal sponsors, had stated during floor debate that "the average system cost methodology worked out by the Bonneville Power Administration should pay the *full cost* of power exchanged by BPA" (*Pacificorp.* 1986, p. 822). BPA's justification for the income tax exclusion was:

> In excluding income taxes from ASC [average system cost] computations, BPA looked to the fact that the IOUs pay income tax because they are organized to make a profit, a characteristic which publicly owned utilities do not share. In reviewing the decision, FERC concluded that it is not necessarily irrational for BPA to decide that BPA's other customers should not have to absorb the costs which the IOUs incur by virtue of their being profit making entities.[*Pacificorp.* 1986, p. 822]

The court of appeals went on to state, however, that "petitioners correctly observe that there is no logical congruence which would support making interest payments on debt a proxy for equity return. There is, as well, an inconsistency in first disallowing equity return and then further disallowing the taxes on such profits" (*Pacificorp.* 1986, p. 823).

The court arrived at the remarkable conclusion that BPA's justification for the change was based on experience rather than on logic. The reason, supposedly, was that the use of "creative financing" by the utilities allowed them to reflect the costs of a utility's investment in a power plant whose construction is terminated prior to its completion in higher equity return allowances. Such procedures are recognized by state regulatory agencies, the court conceded. The Regional Power Act, on the other hand, specifically proscribed the inclusion of terminated plants in the determination of average system costs. The court concluded the matter by stating:

> BPA justifies the substitution of the cost of long term embedded debt for equity return as a way of "capping" BPA's subsidization of profits, in order to enforce the Act's exclusion of terminated plant costs from the ASC subsidy. We cannot hold that its action in this regard is irrational, as it is based upon a justifiable concern about abuse of the program. We therefore conclude that neither the change in ASC with respect to taxes nor the change with respect to equity violated the Act. [*Pacificorp.* 1986, p. 823]

The weak logic of the court emphasizes the economic quicksand upon which it based its decision. A logically superior procedure by BPA would be to determine the actual terminated plant costs and exclude them from average system cost. It is possible that the economic shakiness of the case will lead to further litigation.

Litigation Related to the Rate Ceiling

The original preference customers feared that their rates would be increased as a result of the exchanges. They were brought into the Regional Power Act's compromise by the inclusion in the act of a rate ceiling. The Department of Energy had described this ceiling:

> *Section 7(b)(2)* establishes a rate ceiling for preference customers and Federal agencies which assures that their rates will not exceed what they would have been had BPA not engaged in power sales or purchase transactions with IOU's. Costs that may not be recovered from preference customers are to be recovered from other

customers through other rate schedules. (See Section 7(b)(3).) [U.S. Department of Energy 1981, p. 92]

The Senate report related to the Regional Power Act stated that "the rate limit assures preference agencies their consumers' rates will not be affected, if in the future, IOU costs are higher than anticipated, either through higher financing, construction or operation costs" (U.S. Senate 1979c, p. 61).

The exchange mechanism with the private utilities, as noted, passes on some of the private system costs to the preference customers. It is understandable that they wanted protection against future increases in the costs of the private utilities.

The establishment of the ceiling is another facet of the balancing of interests in the Regional Power Act. The act removed the (hypothetical) possibility that the preference utilities would have to serve the industrial firms if they were deprived of BPA power. The ceiling does protect against the increased costs of the private utilities, but it takes into account the hypothetical costs of the preference utilities serving the industrial firms. The interests of the preference utilities also were served by the regional purchase plan contained in the act that enables BPA to assist the preference utilities in introducing new generating facilities by a mechanism akin to net-billing (billings-credits). The possible savings to the preference utilities on this account must be factored into the ceiling calculation, however.

A host of difficulties are inherent in making such hypothetical calculations. They involve a number of assumptions, predictions, and projections concerning the actual and hypothetical variables involved. An appendix to this report, apparently prepared by BPA, minimized the problems of calculating the ceiling. The appendix states that these specific rate limit factors are objective in nature, although the amount of new resources needed to meet preference customer load growth, including the applicable DSI [industrial customer] load and its costs may require some minor estimating (U. S. Senate 1979c, p. 61).

The appendix did concede that another of the assumptions required in the analysis is far more conjectural. That assumption concerns the troublesome matter of the savings accruing to the preference customers specifically attributable to the regional purchase plan. In other words, the calculations must determine the amount of financial gain to the preference utilities brought about by the act so it can be offset against the increased cost of the private utilities' exchanges.

The appendix presented several sensitivity analyses concerning the variables involved in the rate-ceiling determination to assess their impact on rates. Case studies were made to determine the general effect of variations in load growth, various increases in cost of resources, new preference customers, lower industrial firms loads, increased inflation cost, and raised cost of exchange power. The appendix concluded: "If the IOU annual costs for new resource developments are substantially higher than those of preference customers due to higher interest rates, lower than anticipated tax benefits and higher than expected capital costs, then the rate ceiling triggers in the later years of the analysis after 1994–1995" (U.S. Senate 1979c, pp. 61–62).

If the rate ceiling were to "trigger in," that is, forestall the passing on of some of the exchange costs to the preference utilities, BPA would have to find a mechanism to pass on these costs to its other nonpreference customers, the private utilities or the industrial firms. Challenges to the analyses could be made at any number of points— for example, on the serious question of the various load growths in the future, past predictions by BPA and others concerning future power demands in the region have been notably inaccurate. Another example is the prediction of future inflation; that is a hazardous exercise at best. These are but two of the variables involved in these rather complex analyses. BPA's estimation of any number of other variables could easily come under challenge.

BPA has been taken to court on its rate-ceiling estimation, which is not surprising given the subject's complexity. A trade association representing the preference utilities and one large preference utility challenged BPA on this issue (*Public Power Council* 1984). The case joined several others in being dismissed on procedural grounds. One of the plaintiff's arguments is most interesting, however. They contend that the process for developing a methodology is unfair because BPA will be able to manipulate the methodology as it develops its 1985 rates: "Plaintiffs fear BPA will predetermine how much it wants to charge preference customers and then devise a rate test methodology which allows such charges. They argue that the methodology will be so complex that it will be easily subject to manipulation once BPA knows the numbers involved in the 1985 rate case" (*Public Power Council* 1984, p. 204).

Litigation Related to Other Ratemaking Problems

In 1985, other aspects of BPA ratemaking drew several legal challenges. Three of these challenges came from California buyers of BPA power. These challenges did not arise directly from the preference provisions or the Regional Power Act, but they were indirectly related. The rates charged to Californians have a direct impact on the rates charged to users within BPA's region. The pressures on BPA to raise rates within the region can be eased if higher rates can be charged outside of the region (after all, BPA's operations are supposed to be self-liquidating). The interrelationships between the two sets of pricing policies warrant discussion of the controversies over the prices charged to California users.

The amount of power generated by falling water varies from season to season with differing stream flows. At certain times of the year, power in excess of demands in the Northwest is generated and can be profitably shipped to California. A series of transmission lines known as intertie lines connect BPA's generating facilities to various points in California. There have been long-running disputes over the BPA pricing of this power. In fact, BPA's attempts to pass on large amounts of its costs to Californians antedates the passage of the Regional Power Act of 1980. Californians have insisted that power from federal facilities be furnished to them at the cost of generation. BPA has attempted to charge more than this amount, basing its prices, presumably, on the willingness of the out-of-region users to pay. This dispute was continued in the 1985 case of *California Energy Commission* v. *Johnson*. The gist of the case is:

> CEC alleges that the 1983 nonfirm rates unlawfully discriminate against California ratepayers, and that the rates are based not upon the cost of providing service but with a view toward subsidizing rates charged Pacific Northwest customers. . . . CEC estimates that the 1983 nonfirm rate to be charged California customers during spill conditions is two and one-half to six times greater than that to be charged Pacific Northwest customers. [*California Energy Commission* 1985, p. 633]

Like others previously described, this case was dismissed on procedural grounds.[7] (Spill conditions describe a situation in which there is so much precipitation that water cannot be retained behind

---

[7]Still another case dismissed on procedural grounds involved the Southern California Edison Company of Los Angeles (*Southern California Edison Company* 1985).

restraining dams and must be released. When this occurs, a much larger supply of electricity is generated than is normally the case, at little incremental cost. The power lies in the category of nonfirm power; that is, power that might not be generated with normal or less than normal precipitation and stream flows.)

Two other cases challenge BPA ratemaking decisions during unanticipated power surpluses in 1983 occasioned by extraordinary stream flows. One case was brought by the California Energy Resources Conservation and Development Commission and was decided in 1985. BPA had lowered the rates to two investor-owned utilities to help dispose of the excess power. The court accepted the plaintiff's contention that the appropriate ratemaking procedures were not followed. The majority opinion justified BPA actions, nonetheless, in view of the unusual circumstances facing BPA at the time (*California Energy Resources Conservation and Development Commission* 1985).

In a companion case, also decided in 1985, one of the utilities involved in the previous case sued BPA for reducing the rates to the DSIs without complying with the procedures required by the Regional Power Act. Again, the majority opinion condoned the procedure followed by BPA, citing the unusual circumstances of the time (*Portland General Electric Co.* 1985). Judge Norris dissented in both cases but entered a written dissent in the second case only. His dissent criticized, very sharply, the majority's reasoning:

> For all we know, the twin goals of disposing of surplus power and stimulating the economy of the Pacific Northwest would have been achieved more effectively and equitably if the surplus power had been offered at reduced rates to all BPA customers, not just the DSI's. The point is that the majority opinion that the sales to the DSI's made good economic sense is based on nothing but surmise. [*Portland General Electric Co.* 1985, p. 1485]

BPA's seeming ability to engage in arbitrary pricing policies continues to escape successful legal challenge despite the cogent reasoning of this dissent. It would be interesting to delve more deeply into the bureaucratic motivations for BPA's policies in this regard.

The Regional Power Act's elaborate but tenuous compromise of the various interests has created a number of legal flash points. The principal ones described arise directly or indirectly from the preference provisions, which appear to be most likely issues that will generate litigation.

Litigation Related to Fisheries Provisions

The Regional Power Act assigned responsibilities for the Pacific Northwest's fisheries resources to the newly formed Pacific Northwest Electric Power and Conservation Planning Council, often referred to in shortened form as the Northwest Power Planning Council. Section 4(h) of the act established procedures and authorities to ensure that the fish and wildlife resources in the Columbia River basin would be treated "equitably" in relation to the power-generating and other water resource development purposes of BPA. The intent of Congress was to achieve balance among competing uses of the region's water resources. It established an administrative framework for resolving resource conflicts that may arise because the river network is used to produce fish and wildlife as well as electric power.

The council was charged by the act to adopt a plan with recommendations for fish and wildlife protection. These programs involve both enhancement of these resources and the mitigation of damage to them—for example, by increasing the stock of fish or wildlife. It was believed that the two sets of uses of the water resources tend to be antagonistic. Conversely, increased power generation was seen as interfering with fish reproduction and thereby diminishing the number of fish that can be produced by the fisheries.

The council published its first fish and wildlife program in 1982, followed by amendments in 1984 and 1987. The 1984 amendment repeated the conclusions of the 1982 report with respect to the costs of fish and wildlife protection.

> While initial studies indicate that the Water Budget will reduce firm energy load carrying capacity by approximately 550 Mw [megawatts], the Council itself has not determined the cost of this power loss. The Pacific Northwest Utilities Conference, however, has estimated the cost of replacing 525 Mw of energy loss by various actions. Using conservation and renewable energy resources the estimated cost would be $160 million per year. [Northwest Power Planning Council 1984]

The council continues:

> It is even more difficult to estimate accurately the cost of the capital construction projects, interim water spills, operation and maintenance of the program . . . the Council estimates that if all measures were implemented, the costs would be in the range of approximately $650–740 million over the next twenty years. The

estimate is in 1982 dollars and would result in costs of approximately 0.05 cents per killowatt hour of energy sold by Bonneville. [Northwest Power Planning Council 1984]

The 1987 amended program presented an estimated loss of 550 megawatts but claimed that experience suggested that the actual loss of power would be less. With respect to the estimated $650–$740 million required to implement the fish and wildlife program, the council stated, "The estimate did not include revenue losses to the power system. It also did not reflect the costs of the measures actually adopted." The council promised to study the matter further (Northwest Power Planning Council 1987, p. 26). In other words, the problems of trade-offs between power use and fish and wildlife protection are far from settled.

The latest development as of this writing concerns the licensing of new hydropower sites in the region. This licensing falls within the jurisdiction of the Federal Energy Regulatory Commission.

The U.S. Army Corps of Engineers and the Bureau of Reclamation continue to plan for future federal projects and the Federal Energy Regulatory Commission (FERC), which licenses private and non-federal public power projects, has at least 200 applications to build new dams pending throughout the Northwest. [*Northwest Power Planning Council* 1988, p. 8]

The council is expected to decide in March or April 1989 whether to amend the fish and wildlife program and the 1986 power plan to incorporate the "protected areas" concept. "The protected areas issue refers to designating certain Northwest streams as protected— that is, future hydroelectric development would be restricted— because of the potential impacts on fish and wildlife in those areas" (*Northwest Power Planning Council* 1988, pp. 7–8).

The council, in effect, would be intervening into FERC's decision-making process and possibly impinging on its jurisdiction. The Pacific Northwest Utilities Conference Committee spokesman objected to this possibility. More generally, the series of responses published in *Northwest Energy News* illustrates the significant conflicts between the electric power interests and those favoring fish and wildlife protection. Certainly, the potential exists for future litigation on these issues.

The potential for litigation is enhanced by the vagueness of the Regional Power Act in specifying the appropriate trade-offs between fish and power. The language of section 4(h) of the Regional Power Act states that the fish and wildlife resources are to receive "equitable" treatment, but the act gives no guidance as to what is or what is not equitable. Equity, then, exists in the eyes of the beholder, namely, BPA and the council. It is they who will determine the appropriate trade-offs between these two purposes. Whatever their determination, opposing parties could argue that a different determination is more equitable. Indeed, a particular determination might not receive universal approbation even among the members of one of the opposing parties. Members of the fisheries group seem to differ on the appropriate measures to be taken to preserve the fishery resources.

Given the vagueness of the act, any legal challenge could be credible. Indeed, at least two cases have arisen already: *Forelaws on Board* v. *Johnson* and *National Wildlife Federation* v. *Johnson*. One case was dismissed on procedural grounds, but the other was successful in having an environmental impact statement ordered under the Environmental Protection Act (Northwest Power Planning Council 1983). Given the vigilance of environmentalists and the economic importance of fisheries in the region, it would be very surprising if further legal controversy failed to develop.

Summary and Conclusion

The Pacific Northwest has experienced a steady regimen of legal and economic controversy for two decades or so. The legal controversies have grown directly out of the implementation of public power law and policy in the region. In particular, the preferential rights to federal hydropower greatly complicated the introduction of new power supplies in an economically sensible fashion. The legal rights accruing to the preference utilities would have allowed them to preempt the federal power that had been contracted to the private utilities and the industrial firms. The disfavored power customers of BPA had potentially effective, but untested, defenses to thwart the threatened preemption. BPA, the wholesaler of federal power in the region, attempted an administrative solution to these problems with its hydrothermal programs.

The completion of one nuclear plant out of the five planned and the largest municipal bond default in U.S. history were the legacies of these programs. The legal travail of WPPSS, the organization chosen to build the five nuclear plants, and their participating utilities is still continuing.

Congress attempted a statutory solution to the problems with the passage of the Regional Power Act of 1980. A new set of legal controversy and litigation was set in motion by the act, however. The act embodies a delicately crafted compromise of legal and economic interests among the conflicting claimants to federal power. BPA has been given great authority in power allocation in the region, although this authority is shared by a locally appointed council.

The attempts by BPA to maintain the delicate balances contained in the act have drawn several legal challenges to date. The net result is that the original attempts to avoid legal warfare over public power preference have merely transferred the feared warfare to other battlefields. Whether the legal carnage is less or more than it otherwise would have been is impossible to determine. What is clear is that each attempt to remedy one legal problem arising out of the preference provisions has spawned a host of new ones.

5. Conclusions and Policy Recommendations

Conclusions

Public power policy was the proximate cause of the continuing economic and legal problems of power supply in the Pacific Northwest, at least to the satisfaction of the writer. Public power has not fulfilled its promise of providing electric power widely and inexpensively while pursuing "sound business principles." There is substantial evidence that BPA did not cover its actual costs of operation during most of its history and does not appear to be doing so at this time. Repayment of its obligations to the U.S. Treasury has not been maintained at pledged levels nor has amortization of its debt been made in accordance with ordinary private business practices. The furnishing of power to the rural areas of the region may have served some broad social goal that was worthwhile. But this power has not been furnished pursuant to "sound business principles." This refutes the basic premise of the public power movement that the insistence of private firms on monopoly returns rather than ordinary returns prevented rural electrification. Such electrification could always have been accomplished by taxpayer subsidies.

Public power policy in the region not only contributed to the legal and economic problems of introducing new power supply in the region, it also complicated and impeded attempts to resolve these problems. The hydrothermal programs were attempts to circumvent the difficulties occasioned by the preference provisions. They might have done so had not monumental mismanagement and an adverse ruling of the U.S. Internal Revenue Service intervened. But the point is that the preference provisions had to be circumvented; they could not be abrogated as economic logic demanded.

The Regional Power Act, in its attempt to circumvent the preference provisions, reiterated firmly, if somewhat disingenuously, its fealty to those preference provisions. Although the act did weaken the preference provisions, and thereby went against the spirit of the public power movement, it did expand, enormously, the governmental presence in power planning for the area. The act transformed BPA from a passive wholesaler of power, which was decreed by the original Bonneville Project Act, into a virtual czar of power utilization in the region in conjunction with another local government agency, the Regional Planning Council. Indeed, economic historians might well ponder the fact that a Columbia Valley Authority, which was rejected by Congress during the New Deal era at the apogee of the public power movement, was resurrected by the Regional Power Act in order to resolve problems arising out of public power policy. Irony aside, the important question is whether the expanded role of BPA in allocating electric power use holds promise of resolving and eliminating the problems of the area. Witnesses at the congressional hearings on the Regional Power Act were disturbed at the prospect of a TVA-like agency in the area. Supporters of the act find great merit in the resurrection of the Columbia Valley Authority, however. The following quotations from a policy study at the University of Washington articulate this support:

> The Act embodies several features similar to the Pacific Northwest Regional Planning Board in 1934, and the old Columbia Valley Authority (CVA) proposals, the majority of which appeared during the 1930's and 1940's. The Act has partially resurrected the New Dealer's energy and resource planning vision.
>
> It is not difficult to identify common attributes between the Regional Power Act and the Columbia Valley Authority proposed decades earlier. . . . Also under the CVA proposals, particularly the CVA bills introduced by Senator Warren C. Magnuson and (then) Representative Henry M. Jackson during the late 1940's, the Columbia Valley Authority would have been given the ability to acquire new electric resources, a right eventually granted to the Bonneville Power Administration under the Regional Power Act. And in philosophic perspective, the Regional Power Act's economic efficiency and environmental review criteria are congruent with the CVA concept.
>
> The ability to have a single entity controlling the electric supply system will be instrumental to the success of the regional power plan. The only other region of the country with the degree of single, public entity control over the power supply system to that of the Pacific Northwest is the Tennessee Valley and with a Valley Authority in operation, comprehensive regional power planning already exists. [Olsen and Butcher 1984]

Does the resurrection of the New Deal's energy and resource planning vision really hold promise of resolving the region's energy problems? BPA's performance prior to the act does not augur well for its expanded role. BPA's planning activities in the past have tended to worsen rather than improve matters in the Pacific Northwest. Three major instances can be cited. First, BPA's refusal to follow reasonable pricing policies has tended to increase power demands in the region over those that are economically justifiable. The use of marginal-cost pricing would have cut the power use very substantially. Even the use of average-cost pricing sufficient to cover all costs would have moderated the quantities of power demanded. Second, BPA has consistently misjudged the power demands in the region. Its vigorous promotion of the hydrothermal programs was based on erroneous forecasts of future power demands. Third, BPA's hydrothermal program has been very unsuccessful. Only one nuclear plant was completed and two plants were abandoned. BPA's administrator, Donald Paul Hodel, continued to promote the program even after the Internal Revenue Service withdrew the tax exemption. Hodel's letter was a contributing factor in initiating phase 2, the more disastrous part of the hydrothermal program.

Where is the justification for the great benefits of having a single entity controlling the electric power supply system of the region? BPA did not acquit itself well in its previous planning attempts such as the hydrothermal programs. Even more interesting is the extension of BPA's involvement in the conservation of power authorized by the act. The defenders of the act claim one of its great achievements is the ability to acquire new power resources by the financing of conservation mechanisms and facilities. According to Olsen and Butcher:

> The conservation programs that are the backbone of the regional Council's [Northwest Power Planning Council] plan promise to be much less expensive than would be the conventional approach of building large thermal plants. As envisioned by the Council, resource portfolio development will enable the region to prepare a "least-cost resource mix"—largely composed of blocks of conservation and small scale hydropower units—which can be periodically adjusted to meet actual power demand. [Olsen and Butcher 1984]

It is evident that, in one sense, the use of programs to conserve energy represents the treatment of self-inflicted wounds. The demands for power would have been diminished greatly if BPA had set its rates high enough to recover its costs according to "sound business principles." The higher prices would have compelled the conservation of power by ordinary market forces. (Chapter 3 estimates the extent to which BPA's rates fell short of covering its costs.) These higher rates would have impelled users to economize on the use of electricity without question.

In addition, the schemata developed by the Regional Power Act may well result in an excessive amount of investment in conservation facilities for at least some of the beneficiaries. The ability to transfer costs to BPA may impel investment beyond the amount that would have been undertaken if all of the costs had been borne by the investor in such facilities.

In sum, a belief in the benefits of the comprehensive regional planning for power appear to be based more on hope than on experience in the Pacific Northwest with BPA. Indeed, that experience suggests that alternative policies should be considered.

Policy Recommendations

The above considerations suggest that public power policy has been very unsuccessful in the Pacific Northwest. A multitude of problems appears to have arisen out of those policies and resolution of these problems will come slowly, if at all. In view of this experience, should public power policy be retained in any form in this region? The answer suggested by this study is that power problems will continue to fester in the region unless or until the preference provisions are abrogated. There is a tacit admission of this point in the Regional Power Act, incidentally. That act does, in effect, circumvent the preference provisions. Awareness of that fact led the act's framers to insist that any treatment of the preference provisions in the Pacific Northwest could not be used as legal precedent elsewhere. But to make an explicit abrogation of these provisions would be to admit that the basic premises upon which the public power movement was predicated were erroneous. These provisions were and are, presumably, the line of defense against private power monopolization and exploitation. But public utility regulation and antitrust enforcement have become far more powerful since the 1920s, when the rationale for public power was developed. A more pragmatic defense of these provisions is that they have conferred and will continue to confer significant wealth on the favored preference utilities and their ratepayers. The self-interest of these groups will impel them, understandably, to fight unto the death any weakening of these provisions. Indeed, much of the legal and political wrangling over the years has concerned the maintenance and protection of the preference provisions. Nonetheless, I offer a series of policy recommendations that have as their central feature the elimination of these provisions. My specific recommendations are as follows:

1. The preference provisions of federal legislation should be abrogated with respect to the Bonneville area.

2. BPA should be required to honor all existing contracts. (Pullback provisions would be eliminated with the abrogation of preference provisions.)

3. BPA should offer all available power (after the expiration of existing contracts) on a highest bidder basis. Preference customers should be given the option of meeting any competing offers for the purchase of power.

4. The Regional Power Act should be repealed in its entirety. This would eliminate the billings-credit procedure and abolish the Regional Planning Council.

5. BPA should be required to use replacement cost pricing for its power. BPA should also be required to bring its amortization of debt to the U.S. Treasury in accord with standard business practices concerning debt amortization. At a minimum, BPA should be required to cover all the costs of its operations appropriately calculated.

6. BPA could be entrusted with the management of the fisheries resources of the area, as well as with the other environmental and ecological resources that are related to power generation and use. The provisions in the Regional Power Act in this regard could be adapted to extend BPA this authority. The wording of these provisions, however, should be made much more specific than they are in the Regional Power Act.

The termination of the preference provisions is the beginning and end of all wisdom in the area. Once these provisions are terminated, extensive planning for the area would not be necessary. With federal power being sold to the highest bidder, ordinary market forces will dictate the power use and development of the area. One federal agency in the area should be able to handle the problems that can not be handled well by the market such as the ecological and environmental problems. BPA is the logical candidate despite its past inefficiencies. The functions of the Northwest Planning Power Council would be unnecessary in such a regime.

There is a place for a federal presence in the area, however, because of the ecological and environmental effects of power generation and use. I recommend that power planning be left to market forces and the protection of the environment and the ecology to a federal agency such as BPA.

The Reagan administration made a policy proposal that goes even further in ending BPA's power hegemony in the region. The proposal, made late in 1985, was outlined by the Department of Energy in early 1986:

> Funds are included for operating BPA in FY 1987, but the Administration will actively seek to defederalize BPA by FY 1988. The Administration's position is that although there are historical reasons why BPA was created as a Federal agency, there may no longer be a need for continued Federal operation of this utility system. Utilities are not normally a Federal responsibility and non-Federal owners may be able to operate BPA as efficiently, or more efficiently, than the Federal government. . . .
>
> Although the final terms and conditions of the sale will be developed through a public process, the President's FY 1987 budget estimates assume the Federal power generation and transmission facilities overseen by BPA will be sold at a price equal to the unpaid Federal investment of $8.85 billion on October 1, 1987. The budget assumes payments to the Treasury will be received over four years starting in FY 1988. [U.S. Department of Energy 1986, p. BP–1]

The administration's interim proposal, as outlined by the department, was as follows:

> Although it is expected that BPA will be sold to non-Federal interests, in the interim, legislation is being prepared to modify BPA's capital investment repayment practices. This legislation is expected to protect the interests of the Nation's taxpayers and to be consistent with sound business principles. These modifications require repayment of the unpaid balance of the original Federal investment at a level not less than would be required under a fixed, straight-line amortization schedule for each power investment finances by appropriations and placed in service. [U.S. Department of Energy 1986, p. BP–3]

The proposal was heralded by the administration as a device to lessen the very large federal budget deficit of the time. The elimination of almost $9 billion of that deficit, in addition to its required debt servicing, would certainly lessen budgetary pressures on the federal government. From the standpoint of this study, the proposal's merit is that it would bring a neat and final solution to the electric power problems of the Pacific Northwest and do away with BPA's troublesome financial deficiencies. The interest-rate subsidies would also be eliminated. The private buyer of BPA would have to complete payments for the BPA facilities over a four-year period, and, at the end of that period, the government would have been repaid its full investment in the facilities. The drain on the Treasury occasioned by inadequate amortization and submarket interest rates would be ended.

Depending on the terms of the sale, the end of the continuing legal and economic problems of power supply could also be finally achieved. The sale of BPA would not be conditioned, presumably, on retention of the preference provisions; were it otherwise, the proposal would have to be reexamined. If these rights are fully abrogated, the use of power can proceed along economically rational grounds. Whether companies purchasing the power are publicly or privately owned would not enter into consideration of power distribution. Who gets what would be determined by willingness to pay rather than ownership status.

The policy proposal was met with considerable ridicule and distortion in the national press. Critics likened this proposal to the liquidation of irreplaceable family treasures to pay the family's overdue bills. How can we sell such a family jewel as BPA, asked one prominent economist. What will happen to the salmon that are struggling up the fish ladders, wondered a nationally known columnist.

Although the precise terms of the sale were not specified in the policy proposal, it seems extremely unlikely that title to the national treasures, the dams themselves, would be transferred to private owners. Nor was there any suggestion that the federal government would abdicate its responsibilities for the fish and wildlife in the area, either under the Environmental Protection Act or under other statutes. The commentators in the press made no mention of the value of the proposal in ending the continuing drain on the Treasury, nor of the benefits that would flow from an economically rational use of power in the region. Consequently, there was no talk of putting the treasures to work for the benefit of the entire family, that is the taxpaying public as a whole.

In Congress, the Reagan administration's proposal met a storm of opposition. Indeed, Congress not only rejected privatization but also adopted a resolution that the proposed privatization of BPA (and other power administrations) could not even be studied by the administration. Even the interim proposal to accelerate amortization has not been pursued. (See the discussion of BPA's repayment practices in chapter 3.)

Epilogue

The conclusion of this study, as stated above, is that the codification of public power policy lies at the root of the variegated electric power problems in the Pacific Northwest. In particular, the preference provisions created legal and economic controversies that have afflicted the region for many years. A question posed at the beginning of this study remains to be answered, however. Did the perceived failure of public power policy occur because it was inherently flawed or because of the faulty implementation of that policy? Was it a failed policy or a policy failure?

It is important to discriminate between these two questions because of the policy implications involved. If the original policy was a sound one but was marred by faulty implementation, that policy might be salvaged by improved implementation. If, however, the original policy was basically flawed, the only remedy is to discard that policy and search for alternatives.

The answer that emerges from this study is that public power policy in the Pacific Northwest carried with it the seeds of its own destruction, no matter how well it could have been implemented. It is true that BPA displayed administrative ineptness on several occasions such as its dogged pursuit of the ill-fated hydrothermal program phase 2. But even more adroit implementation could not have corrected for the economic illogic contained in the original policy. Indeed, this illogic led to the problems that have been experienced.

For one thing, the policy was premised on the notion that monopoly powers of the private utilities had prevented the furnishing of electricity to rural and sparsely settled areas. This implied that these power users could be supplied if the profit motive was removed and the costs of provision were covered by a government agency.

BPA's experience appears to confirm the fallacy of this notion. The agency has not covered its costs throughout much of its history.

In other words, power users in the Pacific Northwest have had their power provision subsidized by the American taxpayers.

A second example of economic illogic is contained in the preference provisions. The ability of the preference utilities to preempt the supplies of federal power from the private utilities and industrial firms introduced significant rate disparities among the different power users in the region. Such rate disparities were not based on cost differentials or other economic considerations. This economic illogic spilled over into the legal and political spheres as the disfavored users threatened to avail themselves of preference rights.

The Regional Power Act attempted to preserve the essence of public power policy while circumventing its most troublesome provisions. The act brought a short-range solution to the problems of the 1970s, but the attempted circumvention of the preference provisions has provoked considerable litigation concerning the act. Even more seriously, for the nation as a whole, is the fact that subsidies to the users of electric power in the Pacific Northwest are continuing.

A long-range solution to these problems would seem to involve the discarding of existing public power policy in the region. The policy proposals advanced either by the writer or by the Reagan administration would accomplish this goal.

Neither of these proposals appears to hold much promise of being adopted at the present time, however. Why, then, does this study conclude with policy recommendations that hold little promise of being adopted? First, the recommendations seem eminently sensible based on the findings of this study. Second, policy recommendations that are cavalierly dismissed at one point in time may gain acceptance later. Transportation deregulation and income tax reform, for example, were notions that languished for many years before gaining acceptance. I can only hope that this study will add its weight to other studies and help achieve well-advised reform of the power situation in the Pacific Northwest.

References

Aluminum Company of America v. *Central Lincoln Peoples' Utility District*, 104 S.Ct 2472 (1984).

Anderson, D. Victor. 1985. *Illusions of Power: A History of the Washington Public Power Supply System (WPPSS)*. New York: Praeger Publishers.

Arizona Power Pooling Associations v. *Morton*, 527 F.2d 721, 727–28 (9th Cir. 1975), cert. denied 425 U.S. 911.

Blumm, Michael C. 1983. "The Northwest's Hydroelectric Heritage: Prologue to the Pacific Northwest Electric Power Planning and Conservation Act." *Washington Law Review* 58 (April): 175–244.

Bonneville Power Administration. 1981. *Columbia River Power for the People: A History of Policies of the Bonneville Power Administration*. Portland, Oreg.

BPA. See Bonneville Power Administration.

California Energy Commission v. *Johnson*, 757 F.2d 631 (9th Cir. 1985).

California Energy Resources Conservation and Development Commission v. *Bonneville Power Administration*, 754 F.2d 1470 (9th Cir. 1985).

Central Lincoln People's Utility District v. *Johnson*, 686 F.2d 708 (9th Cir. 1982).

Chemical Bank v. *Washington Public Power Supply System*, 99 Wash. 2d 772 (1983), and *Chemical Bank* v. *Washington Public Power Supply System*, 102 Wash. 2d 874 (1984), cert. denied 105 S.Ct. 2140 (1985a) and 105 S.Ct. 2154 (1985b).

City of Santa Clara v. *Andrus*, 572 F.2d 660, 670–71 (9th Cir.) 1978, cert. denied 439 U.S. 859 (1978).

City of Springfield v. *Washington Public Power Supply System*, 752 F.2d 1423 (9th Cir. 1985) affirming in part *City of Springfield by and Through Springfield Utility Bd.* v. *Washington Public Power Supply System*, D.C., 1983, 564 F.Supp 90.

Degginger, Grant. 1984. "*Chemical Bank* v. *Washington Public Power Supply System*: An Aberration in Washington's Application of the Ultra Vires Doctrine." *University of Puget Sound Law Review* 8:59.

Forclaws on Board v. *Johnson*, 743 F.2d 677 (9th Cir. 1985); *Forclaws on Board* v. *Johnson*, 709 Fed. 1310 (9th Cir. 1983).

Friedman, Milton, and Rose Friedman. 1980. *Free to Choose*. New York: Harcourt Brace Jovanovich.

Fungiello, Philip J. 1973. *Toward a National Power Policy*. Pittsburgh: University of Pittsburgh Press.

General Accounting Office. 1978. *Region at the Crossroads—The Pacific Northwest Searches for New Sources of Electric Energy*. Washington, D.C. EMD 78–76.

_____ . 1979. *Impacts and Implications of the Pacific Northwest Power Bill.* Washington, D.C. EMD 79-107.

_____ . 1981. *Policies Governing the Bonneville Power Administration's Repayment of Federal Investments Need Revision*. Washington, D.C. EMD 81–94.

_____ . 1982. *Bonneville Power Administration and Rural Electrification Administration*

Actions and Activities Affecting Utility Participation in Washington Public Power Supply System Plants 4 and 5. Washington, D.C. GAO/EMD 82–105.

_____ . 1983. *Policies Governing the Bonneville Power Administration's Repayment of Federal Investments Still Need Revision.* Washington, D.C. GAO/RCED 84–25.

_____ . 1986. *Federal Electric Power: Pricing Alternatives for Power Marketed by the Department of Energy.* Washington, D.C. GAO/RCED 80–186 BR.

Hellman, Richard. 1972. *Government Competition in the Electric Utility Industry.* New York: Praeger Publishers.

Kahn, Alfred E. 1971. *The Economics of Regulation. Vol. II: Institutional Issues.* New York: John Wiley & Sons.

Klahn, Jim. "Whoops Trial War." *Arizona Republic,* Apr. 10, 1988.

Leighland, James, and Robert Lamb. 1986. *WPP$$: Who Is to Blame for the WPPSS Disaster?* Cambridge, Mass.: Ballinger Publishing Co.

Lowitt, Richard. 1984. *The New Deal and the West.* Bloomington: Indiana University Press.

Merk, Frederick. 1978. *History of the Westward Movement.* New York: Alfred A. Knopf.

Morison, Samuel Eliot. 1965. *The Oxford History of the American People.* New York: Oxford University Press.

Myhra, David. 1984. *Whoops!/WPPSS: Washington Public Power Supply System Nuclear Plants.* Jefferson, N.C.: McFarland & Co.

National Wildlife Federation v. *Johnson* (D. Or. 1982), 548 F.Supp. 708, affirmed 709 F.2d 1310.

Northwest Power Planning Council. 1982. *Columbia River Basin Fish and Wildlife Program.* Portland, Oreg.

_____ . 1983. *Northwest Conservation and Electric Power Plan, Vol. 1.* Portland, Oreg.

_____ . 1984. *Columbia River Basin Fish and Wildlife Program.* Portland, Oreg.

_____ . 1986. *Northwest Conservation and Electric Power Plan, Vol. 1.* Portland, Oreg.

_____ . 1987. *Columbia River Basin Fish and Wildlife Program.* Portland, Oreg.

_____ . 1988. *Northwest Energy News* 7, no. 2 (April).

Office of Management and Budget. 1985. *Testimony of the Honorable David A. Stockman, Director, Office of Management and Budget, before the Committee on Interior and Insular Affairs, Subcommittee on General Oversight Northwest Power and Forest Management, U.S. House of Representatives.* Washington.

Olsen, Daryll, and Walter R. Butcher. 1984. "The Regional Power Act: A Model for the Nation?" *Washington Public Policy Notes* (Winter).

Pacificorp. v. *Federal Energy Regulatory Commission,* 795 F.2d 816 (9th Cir. 1986).

Pacific Power and Light v. *Bonneville Power Administration,* 795 F.2d 810 (9th Cir. 1986), affirming *Pacific Power and Light* v. *Bonneville Power Administration,* 589 F.Supp. 539 (D. Or. 1984).

Portland General Electric Co. v. *Johnson,* 754 F.2d. 1475 (9th Cir. 1985).

Public Power Council v. *Johnson,* 589 F.Supp. 198 (D. Or. 1984).

Public Utility Commissioners of Oregon v. *Bonneville Power Administration,* 767 F.2d 622 (9th Cir.) affirming *Public Utility Commissioners of Oregon* v. *Bonneville Power Administration,* 583 F.Supp. 752 (D. Or. 1984).

Schlesinger, Arthur M., Jr. 1960. *The Politics of Upheaval.* Boston: Houghton Mifflin.

Shattuck, Richard. 1984. "A Cry for Reform in Construing Washington Municipal Corporation Statutes." *Washington Law Review* 59:653.

Southern California Edison Company v. *Federal Energy Regulation Commission,* 770 F.2d 779 (9th Cir. 1985).

Tamietti, Robert L. 1984. "Chemical Bank v. Washington Public Power Supply System: A Case of Judicial Meltdown." *Journal of Energy Law and Policy* 5:2.

U.S. Department of Energy. 1981. *Legislative History of the Pacific Northwest Electric Power Planning and Conservation Act*. Portland, Oreg.

———. 1986. *Bonneville Power Administration: Budget for the Fiscal Year 1987*. Washington, D.C.

U.S. Department of Energy, Bonneville Power Administration. 1978. *1977 Annual Report*. Portland, Oreg. (June).

———. 1979a. *1978 Annual Report*. Portland, Oreg. (January).

———. 1979b. *1979 Annual Report*. Portland, Oreg. (January).

———. 1981. *1980 Program and Financial Summary*. Portland, Oreg. DOE/BP–43 (March).

———. 1982. *1981 Annual Report*. Portland, Oreg. DOE/BP–100 (January).

———. 1983. *1982 Annual Report*. Portland, Oreg. DOE/BP–152 (February).

———. 1984. *1983 Annual Report*. Portland, Oreg. DOE/BP–205 (February).

———. 1985a. *1984 Annual Report*. Portland, Oreg. DOE/BP–385 (February).

———. 1985b. *Revenue Requirement Study*. WP–85–FS–BPA–07 (May).

———. 1986a. *Bonneville Power Administration 1985 Program and Financial Summary*. Portland, Oreg. DOE/BP–604 (April).

———. 1986b. *Draft WNP 1 and 3: 1987 Resource Strategy*. Portland, Oreg.

———. 1987. *1986 Annual Report*. Portland, Oreg. DOE/BP–793 (March).

U.S. Department of the Interior, Bonneville Power Administration. 1976. *1975 Annual Report*. Portland, Oreg.

U.S. House. 1977. *Pacific Northwest Electric Power Supply and Conservation, Hearings before the Subcommittee on Water and Power Resources of the Committee on Interior and Insular Affairs on H.R. 9020, 9664, 5862*. 95th Cong., 1st sess., pts. 1–5.

———. 1978. *Pacific Northwest Electric Power Issues, Hearings before the Subcommittee on Water and Power Resources of the Committee on Interior and Insular Affairs on H.R. 13931*. 95th Cong., 2d sess., Serial 95–193.

———. 1979. *Pacific Northwest Electric Power Planning, Hearings before the Subcommittee on Energy and Power of the Committee on Interstate and Foreign Commerce on H.R. 3508, H.R. 4159*. 96th Cong., 1st sess., Serial 96–70.

———. 1980a. Committee on Interstate and Foreign Commerce. *Pacific Northwest Electric Power Planning and Conservation Act, Report together with Minority and Additional Views (To accompany S. 885)*. 96th Cong., 2d sess., H. Rept. 96–976, pt. 1.

———. 1980b. Committee on Interior and Insular Affairs. *Assisting the Electrical Consumers of the Pacific Northwest Through Use of the Federal Columbia River Power System to Achieve Cost-Effective Energy Conservation, To Encourage the Development of Renewable Energy Resources, To Establish a Representative Regional Power Planning Process, To Assure the Region of an Efficient and Adequate Power Supply, And for Other Purposes. Report together with Supplemental, Additional, Separate and Dissenting Views*. 96th Cong., 2d sess., H. Rept. 96–976, pt. 2.

U.S. Senate. 1978. *Pacific Northwest Electric Power Supply Act, Hearings before the Committee on Energy and Natural Resources on S. 2080, S. 3418*. 95th Cong., 2d sess., Publication no. 95–154, pts. 1 and 2.

———. 1979a. *Pacific Northwest Electric Power Planning and Conservation Act, Hearings before the Committee on Energy and Natural Resources on S. 885*. 96th Cong., 1st sess., Publication no. 96–28.

———. 1979b. Committee on Energy and Natural Resources. *Pacific Northwest*

Power Planning and Conservation Act. Report (To Accompany S. 885). 96th Cong., 1st sess., S. Rept. 96–272.

Wohabe, David P. 1984 "Chemical Bank v. Washington Public Power Supply System: The Questionable Use of the Ultra Vires Doctrine to Invalidate Government Take or Pay Obligations." *Cornell Law Review* 69: 1094.

About the Author

David L. Shapiro is adjunct professor of economics at San Jose State University. He formerly served as director of the Division of Regulatory and Competitive Analysis in the Department of Energy and has taught economics at San Francisco State University, Arizona State University, the University of Miami, and UCLA. He holds a law degree from the Detroit College of Law and a Ph.D. in economics from the University of California at Berkeley.